The Railways of Britain

18

The Railways
of Britain

O. S. NOCK

B. T. BATSFORD LTD LONDON

First published 1947
First paperback edition 1962

Revised edition © O. S. Nock, 1962

PRINTED AND BOUND IN ENGLAND BY
HUNT, BARNARD AND CO. LTD., FOR THE PUBLISHERS
B. T. BATSFORD LTD.
4 FITZHARDINGE STREET, PORTMAN SQUARE, LONDON W.1

Preface

When the First Edition of this book was published The Railways of Britain had just been nationalised. Most people with a friendly and sympathetic interest in this great industry felt that following the ravages of war the very nadir of its fortunes had been touched, and that already the long climb out of that intense depression had begun. But with conditions in the country as a whole returning to normal, with ample supplies of petrol, and the motor industry gearing up to unprecedented heights of productivity, competition, which had been serious between the wars began to assume the most formidable proportions, and the unification of the railways under national ownership did not yield the economies that had been promised. Unremunerative services were cut; lines were closed, and even the great scheme of modernisation, launched in 1955 has so far failed to turn the tide that seems still to be running so strongly against the railways.

All in all it is a very different railway system of which I have now to write: a system in the midst of the most complete transformation that could be imagined. And yet with all the influx of diesel locomotives and railcars, with the changes wrought by main line electrification, the tradition of the railway service is still firmly based on the traditions of safety and security built up in the past, and upon a pride in the achievements of the steam locomotive. More than this, the memories of the old companies of pre-grouping days are being kept alive by perpetuation of some of the old names, such as "Caledonian", "Great Eastern", "Great Northern", and by the preservation of historical locomotives, rolling stock and other relics—in many cases restored to the original styles of painting.

The section of the general public taking a sustained and detailed interest in the operation and history of the railways has increased ten-fold since the first edition of this book appeared, and the number of railway societies, and model railways clubs that has sprung up all over the country is little short of phenomenal. Yet today it would seem the railways have some new enemies, as well as many new friends, and the activities of the Railway Conversion League, which quite seriously advocates the conversion of *all* railways, including the most intensely used electrified suburban lines, into motor-ways, are not to be regarded lightly. The fact that they have but little practical knowledge of railways does not make their attack any the less serious or enthusiastic!

So from one reason or another this book, like the railways themselves has undergone a very considerable change. Not indeed until I came to read the original text with a view to bringing it up to date did I realise anew how swiftly some of the changes have come upon us. But I could not read once more the original text without recalling the many interesting, forthright, and exciting discussions I had with the late Harry Batsford during the preparation of the book, nor the way I used to leave the offices at North Audley Street often amused, and always exhilarated by contact with his intensely vigorous personality. Naturally one falls to wondering how he would have regarded the events of today. His views on the Railway Conversion League would certainly have been worth hearing!

20 Sion Hill, Bath   O. S. NOCK

Contents

Acknowledgment

The Author and Publishers wish to thank the following for permission to reproduce the illustrations included in this book:

Aerofilms & Aero Pictorial Ltd. for fig. 20; Messrs. Ian Allan Ltd. for figs. 17, 18, 32 and 33; British Railways for figs. 1, 2, 5, 6, 11, 12, 13, 14, 15, 16, 23, 24, 25, 30, 31, 34, 36, 37, 38, 39, 40, 42, 43, 44, 45, 46, 48 and 49; Mr. M. W. Earley for figs. 7 and 35; Mr. J. C. Flemons for fig. 8; The Institution of Mechanical Engineers for fig. 3; Mr. Ian S. Pearsall for fig. 19; Mr. Ivo. Peters for fig. 9; Real Photos Ltd. for fig. 10; Westinghouse Brake & Signal Co. Ltd. for figs. 21, 22, 26, 27, 28, 29, 41 and 47.

The photograph reproduced on the cover of the book is from a colour transparency kindly loaned by Metropolitan-Cammell Carriage & Wagon Co. Ltd.—the designers and mauufacturers of Diesel Pullman trains for British Railways.

List of Illustrations

1

Railway Heritage

THERE was a time, not so many years ago, when persons living in Great Britain who had never travelled by train were very few and far between. It was so, indeed, at the time the first edition of this book was published. Since then however, the enormous increase in the number of private motor cars has led to the rise of a generation among middle-class families that reached prep-school age before travelling in a train. Nevertheless to most of us railways are one of the commonplaces of life, yet many of the most regular and experienced travellers are scarcely aware of the complex organisation that renders their journeys free of incident, still less of the ramifications of the railway service as a whole. We may be acutely conscious of one tiny part of it; some will know by heart the daily service to and from business, with its variations on Sundays and half-holidays, traders will be familiar with particular freight workings, and so on. But apart from such specialised local knowledge railway operation is a closed book for many people; that is where the existence of such a "book" is realised at all. In the diversity of ways in which they serve the country the railways might well be said to render a silent service, for it is usually not until some interruption occurs that the service is realised and appreciated. The late running of a particular passenger train may prove a personal inconvenience, but one is apt to take wholly for granted the regularity in flow of goods, mails, coal and newspapers. In most places indeed there is little outward sign of the vastnesses of the British railway industry as a whole. At the present time the nationalised railways, because of their insolvency, are suffering from a continuous barrage of adverse criticism; but the fact that so much of this criticism is irrelevant and ill-informed is due largely to the unfamiliarity with the railway organisation as it is today—by organisation I refer here to operation, rather than top management.

Some 550,000 persons are employed on the railways of Great Britain. This is 100,000 less than in 1948, but even so it is roughly double the combined pre-war strength of the Royal Navy and the Regular Army! Railways represent not only a great industry, but also a great heritage; a priceless, indispensable national asset, of which the country became acutely aware in the second World War. But in rendering an immense service to Britain herself, and to the Allied cause in general, the railway industry was not merely concerned in the running of the trains. Some of the dramatic incidents of the war themselves give an occasional glimpse into other railway activities. Railway-owned steamers did yeoman work in the evacuation from Dunkirk, and the return to Normandy four years later; railway-owned docks at Southampton, Hull, Liverpool, Cardiff and elsewhere took some of the heaviest bombings of the 1940–1 blitz. Before nationalisation and before they were transferred to a different national authority the British railways owned docks at no less than 76 places, and today the railways operate 130 ships. Important adjuncts to the main business of transport are the hotels adjacent to many of the large stations, while before nationalisation road transport services had been developed as feeders to the main lines, for both passenger and goods traffic.

The modern equipment of the British railways in its very diversity forms an absorbing study; leaving out of account such specialised auxiliary concerns as the steamers, railway engineering proper covers a vast field, from the control of river-flow, protection against the sea and humdrum questions of boundaries and fences, to the building of locomotives, the working of automatic telephone exchanges and the printing of tickets. Operating methods have been developed to meet the growth of business and the increased speed of the trains, and a good deal of this development has been haphazard. But there is evidence now that in railway operation scientific approach to difficult problems is gradually replacing the somewhat hasty improvisations often made in the past. In no field more than that of traffic operation is research needed today, for our crowded tracks have not the best of reputations for punctual running.

The standard of express passenger train services between London and the provinces is high. One can travel to most of the important centres at overall speeds of 55 to 60 miles per hour, including cities so far distant as Edinburgh and Glasgow. The big towns lying amid the Pennines are perhaps among the worst off so far as speedy connections with London was concerned; but in their case the nature of the country and their situation away from any of the trunk routes to the south, amply explains why towns of the size of Halifax, Blackburn and Bolton cannot be reached from London at higher average speeds than 45 m.p.h.

Most cross-country services show overall speeds comparing poorly with the best London trains. Take the case of Sheffield and Bristol: the route is direct and the line well laid out for speed—indeed some fast running is regularly made between the stops. The trouble was that there *were* so many stops; Chesterfield, Derby, Burton-on-Trent, Birmingham, Cheltenham, Gloucester, and usually Mangotsfield as well. At stations like Derby and Birmingham a halt of even five minutes is cutting things pretty fine, and so the overall journey time becomes lengthened to something well out of proportion to the speeds attained intermediately. On a typical through express of today, the "Devonian" the time for the $166\frac{1}{2}$ miles from Bristol to Sheffield is 4 hr. 11 min., an average of only $39\frac{1}{2}$ m.p.h.; of this time 33 minutes is spent standing at intermediate stations. The overall times are still slower on trains using the west to north route, via the Severn Tunnel, Hereford and Shrewsbury. The crack express from Liverpool to Torquay for example averages only 34 m.p.h. on its run of 278 miles. Both these trains are now slower, even, than the corresponding services operating between the two world wars.

Things become even worse should one essay a journey off the organised cross-country routes. At one stage in the writing of this book I thought of making a trip from my wartime home at Chippenham to Malvern, to discuss certain points with Mr. Batsford. There was a reasonably direct line; Great Western to Bath, then over to the L.M.S. and continuing through Mangotsfield, Gloucester, Ashchurch and Tewkesbury. But after consulting Bradshaw, I thought better of it! As the crow flies the distance is about 47 miles. By rail the distance is 83 miles, and the first train in the morning leaving Chippenham at 7.55 a.m. would have landed me in Malvern at 1.10 p.m. with just fourteen minutes to catch the last train back! This latter provided the fastest service of the day between the two towns, 3 hrs. 56 min., giving the startling overall average of just 21 m.p.h. Admittedly this was in wartime, but even in 1938 the best one could do was 3 hrs. 10 min.

Nowadays many journeys that were just possible before the war cannot be made by rail at all, due to the closing of a considerable number of branch lines that had long since ceased to pay their way. Nevertheless some of these hitherto sleepy, cross-country routes leading from the Midlands to the south coast proved of tremendous strategic importance during the war. In readiness for D-day they were re-equipped with modern signalling, additional and lengthened loops, while numerous spur lines were laid in so that heavy goods traffic could readily pass on to them from the main lines leading to London. Thus there flowed an almost ceaseless procession of trains to the ports of embarkation: from the old Great Central, through Banbury and Oxford, on to the Didcot, Newbury and Southampton line; and from the west of England main line of the L.M.S. at Cheltenham there was a parallel flow, over the one-time Midland and

South-Western Junction line, through Cirencester, Swindon, Marlborough and Andover to Southampton. I may add that in the four weeks following D-day there were run no less than 17,500 special trains conveying troops, stores and equipment for the army in Normandy, and 113 trains carrying mails to those same forces—all this in addition to the very heavy traffic scheduled in the ordinary goods and passenger time tables.

But the circumstances of war transport are of course entirely exceptional, and returning to the conditions of 1938–9, it is to note the profound change that had come over railway operation since the outbreak of the first World War. In 1914 the railways had an almost complete monopoly of transport throughout the country. Purely local competitive services were being operated by electric trams and motor omnibuses, but these activities were not extensive enough to affect railway receipts. In the last twenty-five years the development of road services for both passengers and goods, combined with the general depression in trade that was so dominant a factor during most of the time between the wars, has entirely altered the circumstances under which the railways are operated.

From an engineering and operating point of view these periods, first of retrenchment, and then of intense competition, have been not without profit. The times have acted as a stimulus to research in many directions, and from these investigations there has emerged, little by little, a fairly clear picture of both the strong and the weak places in the general scheme of transportation by rail. The railways are pre-eminently suited to the conveyance of heavy loads at high speed over long distances. Against the long drawn out cross-country journey from Liverpool to Torquay, can be set the swarm of heavily patronised business-men's expresses leaving London in the early evening, for Bristol, South Wales, the Midlands and the North, making long non-stop runs at average speeds of 55 to 65 m.p.h.

"Block" loads such as these are obviously an attractive proposition from the operating point of view, and the principle is being applied on an increasing scale, not only in passenger but in goods working. During the war when tracks were so densely occupied it was found particularly advantageous to operate "block" coal trains, for example, from South Wales to the London Area. But the more one comes to examine the details of traffic operation the more one realizes the handicaps imposed by our continued use of loose-coupled goods trains. These may permit of slickness in marshalling, since the shunter with his long pole has merely to slip the link of one wagon over the draw-hook of the next; but any advantage here is nullified tenfold while on the run, particularly where steep gradients are concerned.

I know of an incline $2\frac{1}{4}$ miles long, graded at 1 in 75, down which is operated a large number of heavy goods trains. Each of these trains has to stop at the summit of the bank to pin down the handbrakes on a specified number of wagons, then they crawl down, taking 15 minutes over that $2\frac{1}{4}$ miles. This procedure is followed by another stop of five minutes at the foot of the bank to take off the handbrakes. Thus each descending train spends 33 minutes in covering a critical 4-mile section including that short, though steep incline. If these trains were fitted with continuous brakes an allowance of 8 minutes would be ample. On the other hand, the fitted goods trains, in most cases carrying "block" loads, are run at express speed; so much so, indeed, that whereas in 1938 the palatial "Devonian" averaged only 41 m.p.h. over the 114 miles between the cities of Birmingham and Leeds one could, if on railway business, average 45 m.p.h. over the 111 miles from Peterborough to York by an express goods train! Today steady progress is being made with the equipping of goods vehicles with continuous brakes; but the process is a slow one, and it is to be feared that many years have to elapse before the last of the loose-coupled goods trains runs its course.

The trouble with long distance cross-country services would appear to be that there is normally insufficient traffic to make up the "block" loads that alone would justify running non-stop between the big centres of population, and to enable the "Devonian", for example, to run from Leeds to Exeter calling only at Sheffield, Derby, Birmingham and Bristol. And unless fast and convenient feeder services were arranged one could readily imagine a perfect howl of protest at such an alteration arising from the secondary towns en route; not only from themselves, but also, through their connexions, centres such as Burton-on-Trent, Cheltenham, Gloucester and Taunton which probably contribute almost as much traffic as the large cities.

This book is not, however, purely a treatise on railway engineering and operation. To adopt such a treatment of the subject would be to present altogether too narrow a view of the railways as a national heritage; nor yet does the tale end with the retelling of some of the great stories of constructional days. The romance of travel fascinates each succeeding generation, and there is more even than a wealth of amusement and pleasure to be derived from glimpses of railway working fifty, seventy or a hundred years ago. Such glimpses often throw a vivid light on the customs and manners of the age, as well as giving some insight into the lives of men whose robust faith and indefatigable enterprise sponsored the early railways. Then, as befits a truly British institution, there is a lighter side. The idiosyncrasies of country station staff have been immortalised in *Punch;* trains have provided the setting for comic, as well as breath-taking episodes on stage and screen, but within the railway service itself, quite apart from such tremendous events as the rise and fall of George Hudson, or the catastrophe of the first Tay Bridge, there have occurred many human comedies and dramas stranger and more appealing than some of the wildest flights of fiction. Despite this, there has yet to be written a really great novel of railway life; those authors like Freeman Wills Croft, whose early training and technical knowledge fit them for the task, have so far confined themselves to yarns of mystery and murder. One day perhaps we may have a railway counterpart of "The Citadel".

Certainly the events of 1940–5 would provide any railway novelist with a dramatic background, if he sought one. Countless are the tales of individual acts of heroism, and resource in the blitz; no less amazing are the records of repairs to stations, track, signalling equipment and bridges. A direct hit on a plain piece of line, with the track torn up like a toy and the road-bed heavily cratered meant an interruption of usually no more than eight or ten hours before traffic was running again. The repair gangs did not wait for the all-clear to sound before going out; the trains must run again as soon as possible. Where viaducts were hit the repair work was often a very delicate operation, but some of these incidents were of exceptional interest in showing how magnificently the early railway pioneers had built.

There was the case of the London Road Viaduct, at Brighton, built by John Rastrick in 1845–6. This structure of 27 arches carries the line from Brighton to Lewes at a height of 70 feet above ground level. A heavy bomb from a tip-and-run raider scored a direct hit on one of the piers. Only work of first-class quality would have resisted such an attack without collapsing altogether, and here indeed only the pier actually hit was demolished; the adjoining piers stood firm, while the rails, and even one parapet, hung in mid-air across the gap. The erection of a temporary structure to bridge the gap enabled the line to be re-opened five weeks after the incident, and in four months the viaduct was completely restored.

This incident typifies the spirit of the British railways, past and present: the work of the early engineers, who built so well, and so truly; the organisation of today—for speed on the job would be impossible without the most competent planning; and last of all the spirit of the rank and file of railwaymen, who always "go to it" with such a will in cases of dire emergency. The tradition of service is deep set in our railway history, and today springs from the intense loyalty of an earlier generation of men for their companies—the old individual companies prior to the grouping of 1923. This loyalty manifested itself in many ways; in the spotless turnout of pre-grouping engines and carriages, and in events such as the locomotive trials between Leeds and Carlisle in 1924.

Scientific testing apart, this latter event resolved itself into a terrific "local Derby". The crews of the London and North Western and Midland engines pitted against each other all lived in Carlisle; what was more, they were relatively near neighbours! The fact that both railways were by then merged into the L.M.S group made no difference; partisanship ran to fever heat, and both sides put up some wonderful running. Quite apart from such matters as locomotive testing the grouping of the railways brought a wealth of new problems. On the L.M.S in particular it was hardly likely that two such powerful and strongly individualistic concerns as the London and North Western and the Midland would shake in together easily.

In this respect the Great Western scored heavily at the time of the grouping, for the absorption of the Cambrian, and the local lines of South Wales had no effect upon the established policy and tradition of the company. Its reputation for speed was epitomised in the "Cornish Riviera Express", which for many years made the longest daily non-stop run in the world—225¾ miles from London to Plymouth at an average speed of 55 m.p.h. In its policy of speeding up train services the Great Western set a fairly hot pace in the "twenties", and its enterprise was crowned by the record-breaking trip of the "Cheltenham Flyer" in June, 1932, when the Swindon-Paddington run was made at an average speed of 81.6 miles per hour from start to stop.

Out of the railway grouping there emerged one great personality, Mr. (afterwards Sir) Nigel Gresley, the Chief Mechanical Engineeer of the London and North Eastern Railway, who proved one of the greatest assets of the British railways during a very difficult time. Britain's one-time supremacy in the realm of railway operation was being seriously challenged by developments in America, in France and elsewhere; not only this, but the whole industry of railways was being challenged within Britain itself. By his bold and imaginative work Gresley much enhanced the prestige of British railways in general, and London and North Eastern locomotives in particular. The mechanical reliability of his engines and his clever idea of the corridor tender made possible the longest regular non-stop run the world has ever seen—393 miles from London to Edinburgh by "The Flying Scotsman". In the new streamline age he built the famous "Silver Jubilee" train, which raised the British speed record to 113 m.p.h. Finally came the "Coronation", running from London to Edinburgh at an average speed of $65\frac{1}{2}$ m.p.h., and providing the fastest start-to-stop run ever regularly scheduled in this country from London to York at 71.9 m.p.h. But Gresley was not merely a great locomotive designer, nor yet a great civil engineer in the broadest sense of the term; above all he was a great railwayman, with a finely developed perception of the tradition and heritage in the railways. In this he is one with that company of great men by whose work and example the tradition of the British railways has been built up. A great project, of which he was one of the leading advocates, the Rugby Locomotive Testing Station, was not completed until 1948. On that plant engines can be tested in carefully-controlled conditions, eliminating all the varying factors of weather, traffic delays, and other incidental hindrances that are often experienced when testing locomotives on ordinary service trains, or even on special trial runs.

Just before the publication of the first edition of this book the railways of Britain were nationalised, and in place of the Big Four, and several smaller joint concerns, the Railway Executive was set up under the supreme authority of the British Transport Commission. Apart from purely railway changes the Transport Act of 1947 placed the hotels and catering departments of the railways under a separate authority, the Hotels Executive, while the docks and shipping were placed under yet another, the Docks and Inland Waterways Executive. So far as the railways are concerned their operation is now organised in six Regions, of which two, the Western and Southern, correspond almost exactly to the former Great Western and Southern Railways. The new London Midland Region includes the English lines of the old L.M.S, but the English lines of the former L.N.E.R. have been subdivided into Eastern and North Eastern Regions. In Scotland the lines of the former L.M.S and L.N.E.R. have been merged in a single Scottish Region. Such is the new order, which inherits traditions extending back well beyond the days of the "grouped" railways, to names like the London and North Western, the Highland, the Midland, and the Great Northern, the memory of which is as vivid today as when black Crewe engines handed over the Scotch expresses to blue Caledonians at Carlisle.

2

Their Extent, and How They Came

IN studying the British railways as a national heritage one must take them, primarily, as they are today—a going concern, of some complexity. As such they display the merits and the failings of many a lesser industry that owes its origin and its continuance to private enterprise. To take them purely at their present commercial value, so to speak, would however be to ignore the second aspect of this great heritage: that in the railways we have one of the noblest monuments imaginable to British engineering skill and industrial enterprise. Such enterprise was at first purely local. Colliery owners in the Bishop Auckland district of County Durham, for example, sought a quicker and cheaper means of getting their coal to Stockton, whence it could be conveyed by coastal shipping to London; from this need came the Stockton and Darlington Railway. Witnessing the great success of this northern venture the merchants of Canterbury sponsored a 6½-mile railway to the Thames estuary at Whitstable. One after another short railways were built all over the country for specific purposes, and with almost complete disregard of all but local interests. There were a few men, like George Stephenson, who had some vision of a future railway network covering the entire country, but their counsel availed little in the early days when the foundations of our present system were being laid.

Considering the piecemeal way in which the system grew the facilities now offered are very comprehensive. Far from there being any master plan, each and every new route projected was liable to drastic alteration to placate local opposition. Some towns, like Stamford, at first refused to have a railway running near. The Stockton and Darlington Railway Bill incurred the vigorous opposition of Lord Darlington because the proposed route ran through one of his fox-covers; to so keen a sportsman such an offence was unpardonable and he denounced the measure as "harsh and oppressive, and injurious to the interests of the country through which it is intended that the railway shall pass". All attempts at conciliation having failed the promoters of the bill decided willy-nilly to go ahead. The opposition sent to Lord Darlington an urgent message, which was conveyed to him while he was actually in the hunting field. Using, it said, the strongest expletives of the time the noble Lord called off the hounds and posted in great haste to London, where he was in time to use his influence to secure the defeat of the bill. In drawing up a revised bill, which was submitted to Parliament later, the promoters were obliged to make a considerable deviation to eliminate his opposition.

Opposition was not by any means confined to prominent landowners, to the citizens of certain towns, or to the comparative dignity of Parliamentary debate. Trouble began more often than not when the preliminary surveys were being made. Reliable contoured maps as we know them to-day were then non-existent, and the engineers had to walk or ride on horseback over the proposed routes to gain a clear picture of the lie of the land before even a rough alignment for the railway could be decided upon. These first railway engineers were not welcomed. Naturally they had to have access to private land, and where permission was not granted the engineer's men usually took things into their own hands, with the result that matters came to blows between gamekeepers and the farmers, and these zealous railway pioneers.

During the Parliamentary enquiry on the Liverpool and Manchester Railway Bill George Stephenson was asked: "Do you suppose it a likely thing to obtain leave from any gentleman to survey his land, when he knows that your men had gone upon his land to take levels without his leave, and he himself found them going through the corn and through the gardens of his tenants, and trampling down the strawberry beds which they were cultivating for the Liverpool market?" To which George Stephenson replied, somewhat drily: "I have found it sometimes very difficult to get through places of that kind". As a consequence of the difficulties encountered many of the early railway surveys were rather sketchily done, and in certain bills opponents having accurate local knowledge were able to make considerable capital out of manifest errors in the surveys.

It is perhaps not generally realized that with many of the earliest public railways the haulage of traffic exclusively by steam locomotives was not contemplated at the time the bills were promoted. The Stockton and Darlington Railway was laid out primarily for horse traction, and for some little time the bulk of the traffic was thus conveyed. The few steam locomotives in service were used for coal trains, and passengers were taken by horse-drawn coaches run by private individuals who paid toll to the company for use of the tracks. There was keen rivalry between the various drivers and many a delicate situation arose when two such coaches happened to meet head-on at a point on the line where there was no passing place; it was not in the nature of these tough old boys to give way!

In view of the long and honourable history of the steam locomotive one is inclined to treat with amusement the early opposition to its use on railways; but while some of this opposition did arise from that blind prejudice which in every age sets itself against any new development, a considerable amount came too from a more careful consideration of the factors involved. The early locomotives were not always reliable; repairs to them took a long time to execute, and accidents sometimes occurred through carelessness in manipulation by the drivers. The Newcastle and Carlisle Railway provided in 1833–4 what was probably one of the last instances of debate as to the type of motive power to be used. The original Act prohibited the use of locomotives, but it was pointed out that a great saving in constructional cost would be possible if steam traction was adopted. Instancing the section between Prudhoe and Hexham, 10 miles long, where it was proposed to lay down a single line, four sidings to the mile would be needed with horse haulage whereas with locomotives one siding would suffice. And this alone would yield a saving of nearly £700 a mile in construction.

The problems confronting railway pioneers have to be viewed against the background of industry in general at that time. Mechanical engineering was in its infancy; the materials available were merely wrought and cast iron, copper, brass and wood, and manufacturing processes were largely confined to those represented by the foundry and smithy. Rails were either cast iron, or short forged bars, often not more than two feet in length. A point that was to prove of immense importance, and moreover not merely to British railways, was settled in a singularly casual way. George Stephenson's first locomotives were built for service at Killingworth colliery, which was connected with the Tyne by a wagonway having a rail gauge of 4 ft. 8 ins. There is evidence to show that this gauge was peculiar to the line. It would seem only natural however that Stephenson when laying out the Stockton and Darlington Railway should adopt the same gauge, as it was also suitable for the proposed passenger coaches. Actually the rails appear to have been laid fractionally wider, and in all subsequent lines with which Stephenson was connected the gauge was 4 ft. 8½ ins.

But while Stephenson's gauge was accepted in most quarters as quite suitable, there are very few matters, even in the realm of engineering, that do not permit of a difference of opinion. And so we come to that colossus of railways, Isambard Kingdom Brunel. This brilliant son of Sir Marc Brunel, Engineer of the Thames Tunnel, was a man whose every conception was on a colossal scale.

At the age of 27 he was appointed Engineer to the Great Western Railway. Having made for that company a magnificent main line from London to Bristol he went on to build the Bristol and Exeter, the South Devon Railway, the Cornwall Railway, and finally the West Cornwall Railway. There were no half measures with Brunel; everything he did was either a colossal success or an equally colossal failure. It was characteristic of him to dismiss the 4 ft. $8\frac{1}{2}$ ins. gauge as inadequate for the traffic of the future, and to adopt a gauge of no less than 7 feet for the Great Western, and the associated railways leading into Devon, Cornwall and South Wales. He determined upon the finest road he could conceive regardless of what other engineers were doing. It would seem that he looked upon railway operation purely in its engineering implications, and such a matter as convenience of interchange with other railways interested him little. A striking instance of this is provided by the Taff Vale Railway which he was building at the same time as the Great Western; although this line would connect at Cardiff with the broad-gauge South Wales Railway Brunel adopted the 4 ft. 8 in. gauge for the Taff Vale, in all probability because it was built mainly as a mineral line and the high speeds he envisaged on the 7 foot gauge would not be required.

By the time the Great Western was under construction work was proceeding apace with other trunk lines. From important local concerns like the Stockton and Darlington, and the Liverpool and Manchester, attention was now becoming focused on altogether larger projects, and the vision of a railway network covering the whole country was beginning to take shape. By the year 1836 work was well in hand on the Great Western—which was then authorised only from London to Bristol—the London and Birmingham, and the Grand Junction, which latter ran northward from Birmingham to a junction with the Liverpool and Manchester Railway near Warrington. The London and Birmingham, and the Grand Junction, important links in the West Coast trunk route to the north, were both products of the Stephenson school. The first to be opened, the Grand Junction, was built by Joseph Locke, a pupil of George Stephenson, and one who had served under him as a resident engineer during the construction of the Liverpool and Manchester Railway. Locke it was who later surveyed and built the Lancaster and Carlisle Railway, that famous road through the Westmorland fell country that for so many years sorely taxed locomotive power. George Stephenson's son, Robert, was Engineer of the London and Birmingham. He was perhaps the most outstanding of all the early railway engineers, for he was not only a master of the constructional side but also a highly successful locomotive designer. His name is borne today by one of the best known British locomotive building firms, Robert Stephenson and Hawthorns Ltd.

Even judged by the standards of today the railways built by Brunel, Locke and the Stephensons would be considered vast engineering works, and one cannot do other than pay homage to the men who essayed such tasks with no mightier tools than picks and shovels, and no means of cartage other than with horses. It is safe to say that the earthworks of these early trunk lines were far greater than if they had been constructed in the "eighties", or in recent years. They were built at a time when the deficiencies of existing steam locomotives in hill climbing were somewhat glaringly apparent. George Stephenson's locomotives had progressed so far from the original Killingworth engines that he included gradients of 1 in 96 on the Liverpool and Manchester Railway; but they proved unexpectedly troublesome.

In 1830 a test was made on the Whiston "inclined plane" with a train load of 33 tons. With two engines coupled on a start was made $\frac{1}{4}$ mile from the foot of the incline, and a speed of 17 m.p.h. was quickly attained. But although the gradient of 1 in 96 lasted for only $1\frac{1}{2}$ miles the two engines only just managed to reach the summit, which they crawled over at 4 m.p.h. With experiences like this in view Robert Stephenson planned the London and Birmingham with no gradient steeper than 1 in 330, except for the final drop at 1 in 70 from Camden into Euston, where locomotives were not at first used. On the Great Western Brunel had no gradient steeper than 1 in 660 in the first 85 miles out of London, and the Grand Junction was built in much the same style.

This easy grading is of inestimable value in the handling of modern traffic, but the implications from the constructional point of view are to be seen in the great cuttings at Tring and Roade (Northants) on the London and Birmingham; in the lofty curving embankment west of Chippenham, and in the Sonning cutting, on the Great Western. In building the first lines to the south coast this same evenness of gradient was preserved,

1 London and Birmingham Railway: building the Boxmoor embankment in 1837, showing the method of conveying material by wheelbarrow

From a drawing by J. Bourne

2   London and Birmingham Railway: a working shaft in Kilsby Tunnel, 1837

From a drawing by J. Bourne

3   Robert Stephenson
From the painting by John Lucas

4   Euston in 1837

From a contemporary print

5   Paddington in the 1930s

6 A Great Northern 0–4–2 decorated for the annual free trip of the Engineers' Department, Hitchin, 1887

7 A Special on the Southern Region: a dynamometer car test run with a rebuilt "Merchant Navy" locomotive

8 Romney, Hythe and Dymchurch Railway: the "Bluecoaster Limited" leaving Dungeness

9 Liverpool and Manchester Railway engine "Lion", built 1838, at Monkton Combe, Somerset, during the filming of "The Titfield Thunderbolt"

10 Metropolitan Railway: one of the first electric locomotives hauling a
Pullman car train from Aylesbury to Moorgate Street

11 A modern local train, London Midland Region: a two-car diesel-
mechanical unit, bound for Shotton

12 A Royal Train of 1902 on the Great Western Railway; hauled by the specially decorated engine "Britannia"; this train was used by King Edward VII and Queen Alexandra for a trip to Plymouth

though locomotive progress had by then suggested a slight relaxation to a maximum steepness of 1 in 250. This figure was observed by Locke in constructing the London and Southampton, and it involved him in some tremendous cutting and embankment work between Basingstoke and Winchester.

The methods used in the excavation of Tring cutting give a very good idea of the prodigious amount of manual labour involved in the building of these early railways. The actual digging was done entirely by hand, but as the depth of the cutting increased a novel method of removing the earth was used. A series of sloping boards were arranged up which the excavated material was lifted in horse-drawn wheelbarrows. The horses moved along the top of the cutting on a line parallel to the course of the railway and the barrows were hauled up by long ropes passing over pulleys. Each barrow had to be guided by a labourer, and a dangerous occupation it was for these men on so steeply sloping a platform. Many a time a jerk by the horse upset the balance of the wheelbarrow, and man and barrow went tumbling down to the bottom of the cutting. Despite this somewhat hazardous method of working there was only one fatal accident during the making of the Tring cutting. This great excavation is $2\frac{1}{2}$ miles long, and in places it is nearly 60 feet deep.

The contractors who undertook these early railway works rarely made much profit out of it. In a job like the Roade cutting, $1\frac{1}{2}$ miles long, in places nearly 70 feet deep through hard rock and clay, there was little or no previous experience to act as a guide, and the difficulties of the task were altogether underestimated. The contractor failed, the railway company had to take over the work, and the eventual cost of this section alone was £130,000 more than the contract price. It was the same at Kilsby Tunnel, 5 miles south of Rugby. Here the trial borings failed to reveal an extensive quicksand, and very soon after construction had been started the roof suddenly collapsed and water flooded the workings. The Stephensons, father and son, took over personal direction of the work, and the tunnel was eventually completed, at a cost of £125 per yard.

Another characteristically awkward job that faced early railway engineers was the crossing of marsh land. George Stephenson came up against it at Chat Moss, on the Liverpool and Manchester Railway, where the line passed over the remains of a belt of uncultivated fen, which at one time extended almost unbrokenly from Lynn to the Mersey. Preliminary surveys failed to find any solid bottom on which an embankment could be built, and so Stephenson tried the experiment of "floating" the railway on a mattress of hurdles interwoven with heather. This mattress was spread over the surface of the bog, and the solid material for the embankment tipped on to the top of it. The mattress sank into the moss. More solid earth was tipped on. For weeks and weeks the work went on without the slightest apparent effect. It seemed impossible to raise the embankment a single inch, and eventually the directors became so seriously alarmed at what they thought was the hopelessness of the task that a board meeting was held on the site, to decide whether or not the work should be abandoned. Stephenson's robust confidence however carried the day, and eventually after a seemingly endless spell of further tipping the bank began to rise, firm and solid.

The earthworks of our railways are now such a commonplace that even discerning travellers scarcely give them a thought. They nevertheless remain some of the greatest if less spectacular monuments to the memory of the early railway enginers. The tunnels, which at the time of their construction gave rise to so much apprehension on the part of ill-informed and biased persons, were mostly adorned with highly decorative entrances. Situated usually at the end of some deep and newly-excavated cutting the effect was certainly enhanced thereby. The growth of vegetation during the past hundred years has mellowed almost out of recognition the harsh grandeur of these railway vistas, and the classic portico of Watford Tunnel and Brunel's castellated entrances to the short tunnels between Bath and Bristol pass almost unnoticed.

But in the half-mile of railway through the Wiltshire village of Box two examples of Brunel's work remain in much of their original splendour. As if to symbolise the magnitude of the task of building the Box tunnel itself, and to accentuate the importance of the railway as a whole he surrounded the west portal with a façade stupendous in its proportions. The arch is nearly twice the height necessary for modern traffic, and the yellowish Bath-stone blends pleasingly with the picturesque hillside rising at the back. When newly-built this tunnel entrance must have provided road travellers with an awe-inspiring sight, for the Bath Road crosses the railway on a high bridge less than a quarter of a mile from the tunnel. For good or ill Brunel certainly advertised the Great Western Railway. One can understand his wishing to put so majestic a finishing touch to the Box tunnel itself, but in what light can his equally grandiose treatment of Middle Hill tunnel be regarded? For this latter is not 200 yards long, and cuts through a spur of the hills between Box station and the main tunnel. Be that as it may, the entrances are second only in size and impressiveness to the west end of the Box tunnel proper.

In the present age, when new works, railway or otherwise, are planned on a purely utilitarian basis, little in the way of ornamentation is employed. It is true that the earliest railways were built in a decorative age, but even so the incidental adornments nowadays seems out of all proportion to the scale of the works as they were then. There was, for example, the great and picturesque Moorish Arch spanning the tracks of the Liverpool and Manchester Railway at Edge Hill, Liverpool; and Philip Hardwick's enormous Doric Arch at the entrance to Euston. They arose, or so it would seem, from a realization by these pioneer railwaymen of the greatness of their enterprise, and from a resolve to crown it with architecture of appropriate majesty. As we now know they built even greater than they knew, and it is to be regretted that in the vast material developments of later Victorian days so many of our important stations were allowed to grow into such gloomy jumbles of buildings, which process is aptly epitomised by the encompassing of the Doric Arch at Euston by so many wholly undistinguished edifices.

The artistry of the earliest railway engineers found its

36

greatest expression when it came to the building of bridges. The even grading of the great trunk lines involved some structures that were considered very large at the time. There was the Wharncliffe Viaduct over the Brent Valley, on the Great Western; the Wolverton Viaduct over the Ouse, on the London and Birmingham, and the viaduct over the Weaver, on the Grand Junction. But in these early railways the routes were carried along more or less obvious courses, through the gently rolling country of southern England. Matters became considerably more interesting when Locke and the Stephensons drove the iron road northward to the Scottish border, and when Brunel got to work west of Exeter.

The Royal Border Bridge, at Berwick-on-Tweed, is a superb example of Robert Stephenson's work. In a beautiful setting between the heights leading to Halidon Hill and the red-roofed town of Berwick it carries the railway high above the winding estuary of the Tweed, the rails being 126 feet above high water mark. The bridge is built partly on a curve, and its twenty-eight warm red arches are finely seen from a northbound train as Tweedmouth Junction station is passed, and the long sweeping curve is entered upon. The Royal Border Bridge was opened in 1850, when locomotive axle-loads did not exceed 12 tons, and the total weight that one of its $61\frac{1}{2}$-foot arches was called upon to support was about 70 tons. The bridge was so robustly built that today locomotives having an axle-load load of 23 tons pass over many times a day, and the greatest weight-concentration on one of those arches may be as much as 150 tons.

In crossing navigable waterways both Brunel and Robert Stephenson were set tasks of exceptional difficulty, and in some ways very much alike. Stephenson's problem was to carry the double track of the Chester and Holyhead across the Menai Straits; Brunel's to carry the broad gauge single track of the Cornwall Railway across the Tamar at Saltash. Both waterways are almost exactly the same width, 1,100 feet, and in both cases the Admiralty would not permit of any navigational obstructions, such as temporary scaffolding, however brief their use might be. Both engineers bridged their respective waterways with viaducts having two main spans; these spans were constructed completely on the adjacent shores and then floated out to a temporary anchorage against the partly completed main piers of the bridge. They were then gradually raised to their full height by hydraulic jacks, the supporting masonry being completed little by little after each successive lift of the main spans. But although the general principle of construction, and the local circumstances, were so much alike the details of the two bridges were entirely different. Stephenson carried the railway inside a wrought iron tube of rectangular section, and the appearance of the completed bridge, though striking, was somewhat severe; Brunel, using for his main spans a combination of an arch and a suspension bridge, took the line from Devon into Cornwall over a structure that for sheer beauty has never been surpassed in bridge building.

There is no doubt that the responsibility for carrying through so great and so novel a work weighed heavy upon Robert Stephenson. Well it might! The larger spans were each 460 feet long, weighing 1,587 tons. His innate caution required the most lavish provision against any kind of mishap, during the difficult operation of floating the tubes into position, while as an additional precaution the tubular girders were made vastly stronger than was then necessary. Stephenson's dictum in the design and building of the Britannia bridge was, that if one chain, one rope or one bolt was amply strong enough for a particular duty two should be provided. So great was the interest taken in the work that two of the greatest railway engineers of the day, Joseph Locke and Brunel himself, acted as volunteer assistants to Stephenson, and were members of the Menai Tubular Bridge Council.

The launching of the first large span on the evening of June 20th, 1849, was a complicated operation, and despite Stephenson's care and forethought it turned out to be a distinctly hazardous one. The tide runs very swiftly in the straits, and the scheme made use of this natural power to carry the tube, at high water, from its moorings, whence it would be guided by cables from the shore and swung into position on ledges in the bases of the towers. As the tide ebbed the tube would be left suspended; the pontoons on which it had been floated could be withdrawn, and the task of raising the tube little by little up the towers could be commenced. The conception was magnificent, and its execution likely to be spectacular.

The operation was originally planned for June 19th, but the weather was unfavourable and Stephenson decided to postpone it for one day, to the disappointment of the many sightseers gathered on both banks of the waterway. Great was the merriment among the engineers next morning when one of the daily newspapers was found to contain a highly-coloured description of how the great tube had been successfully floated into position! The actual operation was carried out "according to plan" on June 20th, with Robert Stephenson personally directing it from the top of the floating tube. There was a minor mishap when one of the capstans broke, but even this slight incident was seized upon for some sensational writings in the press, not the least offender being Stephenson's famous biographer Samuel Smiles.

As Stephenson built so the bridge stands today. To passengers by the Irish Mail it is no more than a vague rumble in the night, while even on the day mails and other expresses the neighbouring village of Llanfairpwll-gwyngyllgogerychwyrndrobwll-Llantysiliogogogoch, with its 25-foot-long station nameboards, receives more publicity than one of the noblest monuments to British engineering genius.

Brunel's superb viaduct over the Tamar is seen to much greater advantage by railway travellers. On the Cornish side of the river the line swings round through a full right angle, so that the delicate tracery of the bridge can be seen in all its beauty against the colourful background of a noble estuary. Having in mind the immense labour and anxiety connected with this bridge, and that over the Menai Strait, one is inclined to ask how the problems set to Stephenson and Brunel would be tackled today, with modern appliances and all this pioneering experience in view. The answer is, I think, to be seen in the great bridge over Sydney Harbour—built out simultaneously from both banks in latticed steel. The Saltash and Menai bridges were built before the days of steel, and before the principle of the cantilever had been demonstrated so strikingly in the construction of the Forth Bridge.

One other great viaduct of the early railway days must be mentioned, that over the Belah glen, near Kirkby Stephen, on the cross-country line from Darlington to Penrith. Mr, afterwards Sir Thomas Bouch was the engineer, and in this wild moorland country he took the railway at a height of 196 feet over the glen on a viaduct of most delicate beauty and distinction. It is remarkable too in that cast and not wrought iron is the principal material used in the towers that support the latticed-iron girders. In the towers wrought iron is used only for the ties. The detailed design which is due not to Bouch but to Robert H. Bow, permitted of very rapid construction, and although built on firm ground, instead of tidal waterways, the time taken to erect the viaduct—only four months—is in extraordinary contrast to the four years taken to build the Britannia tubular bridge, and still more so to the six years spent in the construction of the Saltash bridge.

Belah viaduct is 1,040 feet long, on a lengthy gradient, where the railway is climbing at 1 in 60 to reach the 1,370 ft. altitude of Stainmore summit, all but the highest point reached by any English standard gauge railway. The highest is at Princetown, Devon, Western Region—1,373 feet up. As the train comes pounding up the bank from Kirkby Stephen, working its way round a shoulder

41

of the rolling moorland, the viaduct comes into view, so slender, so exquisitely graceful, that seen amid the broad Pennine landscape it seems a mere fairy thing. Yet Bow and the contractor Gilkes Wilson here built as truly as the Stephensons and Brunel, and their lightning work of 88 years ago today carries a heavy mineral traffic: coal and coke westbound from Durham, iron ore eastbound from Cumberland. The nature of the traffic recalls the name of the original company; this was the South Durham and Lancashire Union Railway, the object of which was to link the Durham coalfield with the industrial districts of North Lancashire and West Cumberland. This line was first absorbed in the Stockton and Darlington, and later became part of the North Eastern Railway. As such it eventually became part of the L.N.E.R. system.

The building of a railway having a lengthy gradient of 1 in 60 to be used by ordinary steam locomotives shows how soon the earlier dictum of Robert Stephenson—no grade steeper than 1 in 330—was swept aside. Yet it is supremely fortunate that the pioneer trunk lines were so magnificently engineered, for this physical characteristic makes much easier the conveyance of the heavy and fast traffic of today. The engineering has its advantages for the traveller, quite apart from the evenness of the speed resulting from such slight gradients. Traversing some of the great embankments opens up broader views and wider prospects than can be enjoyed from the neighbouring roads, panoramas that are usually reserved for the ridge-walker. On the Southampton line, for example, while the train is sweeping down towards Winchester at 75 to 80 m.p.h, mile upon mile of open rolling country is displayed to east and west of the railway. Sir William Cubitt's great viaduct over the Foord gap gives a wonderfully picturesque view over Folkestone and that range of chalk cliffs stretching away towards Dover—cliffs that have become symbolical of England itself. Only by train can one experience that amazing run among and through the chalk cliffs.

No greater contrast between earlier and later trunk lines could be found than between Joseph Locke's smoothly graded route from London to Southampton, completed in 1840, and the Portsmouth "Direct Line", which was opened 19 years later. Until the latter railway was completed passengers from London to Portsmouth had to travel either by the Southampton line as far as Eastleigh, or through Brighton and along the coast. Both were roundabout routes, and the Direct Line took a short cut from Woking through Guildford, Haslemere and Petersfield to join the coast line at Havant. It passed through hilly country; over the eastern spurs of Hindhead, and then, after an abrupt descent, through the South Downs by a tunnel near Petersfield. Here was scope for some stupendous engineering works. Instead however the line was carried uphill and down dale on gradients of 1 in 80, and the only cuttings and embankments were made to smooth out local hillocks and depressions.

As train loads increased it became a terror to the locomotive department, and I have vivid recollections of heavy holiday trains toiling up the 1 in 80 gradients to Haslemere at no more than 15 m.p.h. giving, it is true, ample time to enjoy the bold escarpments of Hindhead, looking out over a rough country of wild upland copses, purple moors, groups of dishevelled pines, and commons golden with gorse in bloom. The speed of trains fluctuated enormously. One morning when I was riding up from Portsmouth on the locomotive of a fast express we chugged our way through the short tunnel under the South Downs at 25 m.p.h. We were a few minutes late, and the driver was in a hurry; with a clear road he just let fly down the succeeding gradient. We swept through Petersfield at 75 m.p.h., and reached no less than 84 at the foot of the incline—an acceleration from 25 to 84 in just five miles of line! Exciting as such fluctuations can be they hardly represent the most economical form of travelling.

By the year 1860 the system of trunk lines as we know it today had definitely taken shape, though not all the companies had completed their expansion. The Midland Railway, one of the largest constituents of the one time L.M.S system, was then no more than an extensive, though certainly very prosperous, local line. It was originally formed in 1844, by amalgamation of three smaller companies: the North Midland, running from Derby to Leeds; the Midland Counties, from Derby to Nottingham with a branch running through Leicester to join the London and Birmingham at Rugby; and the Birmingham and Derby Junction Railway. Derby was thus the focal point of the new company, and it remained the headquarters till 1923, when the final merger took place.

The 72-mile main line of the North Midland was in many ways one of the finest of George Stephenson's works. Running by way of Ambergate, Chesterfield, Rotherham, and Normanton it tapped a rich mining district, and was eventually to become one of the busiest pieces of railway in all England. At the time of its opening it had an even greater significance, for over it was provided the first through railway communication between London and the north-eastern counties; from 1840 through carriages were run from Euston to York, 217 miles via Rugby, Leicester, Derby and Normanton. The Midland Railway, as originally formed, was in the nature of an important connecting link, rather than a trunk line on its own. But the arrangement whereby Euston handled the entire traffic from London to the north could not, at the rate business was developing, suffice for very long, and in 1846 the Great Northern Railway was incorporated, providing a direct line which shortened the distance between London and York to $190\frac{1}{2}$ miles.

Not all the railway schemes projected in these comparatively early days were based on sound policies of traffic development, or yet of pure competition for growing business. There was a period, roughly between the years 1845 and 1848, when the country went "railway mad". The great success of the pioneer lines let loose a torrent of speculative buying of railway shares; worse than that, it led to the promotion of countless new companies of quite specious origin, the directors of which can have little intention of doing anything in the nature of serious railway building. So artificial a boom was followed by the inevitable crash, and in the resultant slump it was not only that the fraudulent promoters and the luckless small investors were ruined; public confidence was so severely shaken that the well-established companies and many genuine new schemes suffered a recession from which they never recovered—at any rate to a prosperity such as had been enjoyed prior to 1845.

During this period of the Railway Mania, as it has been called, one great personality stands out, that of George Hudson. In an article written many years after he had passed from the railway scene the *Newcastle Chronicle* aptly sums up his meteoric rise to fame and fortune: "At the beginning of the railway system we find him a modest draper, doing a quiet business in the cathedral city of York, with nothing to distinguish him from the rank and file of shopkeepers. Railways became the passion of the hour, and the York draper was bitten by the mania. Mr. Hudson risked all and was successful. Stimulated by success, he played again; again fortune proved propitious. His name became an authority on railway speculation, and the confidence reposed in him was unbounded. For a time the entire railway system of the North of England seemed under his control. What herculean energy was in the man may be gathered from a couple of day's work, under Mr. Hudson's direction. On the 2nd of May, 1846, the shareholders of the Midland Company gave their approval to 26 bills which were immediately introduced into Parliament. On Monday following, at ten o'clock, the York and North Midland sanctioned six bills, and affirmed various deeds and agreements affecting the Manchester and Leeds, and Hull and Selby Companies. Fifteen minutes later he introduced the Newcastle and Darlington Company to approve of seven bills and accompanying agreements; and at half-past ten took his seat as a controlling power at the board of the Newcastle and Berwick. In fine, during these two days he obtained the approval of forty bills, involving the expenditure of about £10,000,000. For three years matters went bravely on, each succeeding day being a witness of greater wonders than its predecessor."

The purely local interests which had given rise to the earliest railways were still very much to the fore. The Midland, the York and North Midland, the Newcastle and Berwick, and others, were by their very names little more than local lines; but Hudson was the co-ordinating genius that so directed the policies of the various companies as to weld their interests together, and lead them towards the building up of one great system serving the whole of north-eastern England. The Midland provided the link to the South, and by the autumn of 1848 one could travel by rail the entire way from London to Edinburgh, via the east coast route. It is easy to see however that no matter how great the benefits bestowed upon posterity through the building up of this railway system it was Hudson himself who stood to gain most at the particular moment; and while all was going well no one grudged him the immense personal fortune he was amassing. That he was a man of very high intellect goes almost without saying; that he had a breadth of vision, and immense self-confidence is freely granted too. Indeed in 1848 he appeared to be within an ace of becoming the greatest railway personality in the whole country.

But unfortunately his integrity was not of the highest. Even in the years of great prosperity there had been some directors and shareholders, ordinarily cautious men and addicted to none but strictly orthodox methods, whose consciences had been mildly stirred by some of Hudson's transactions, but who in deference to the evident satisfaction with the state of affairs expressed by the great majority of the shareholders did not then raise their voices. But when at the end of 1848 the bursting of the Railway Mania "bubble" sent tumbling the dividends of even the soundest concerns, questions began to be asked, and a point raised in February 1849 at the half-yearly meeting of the York, Newcastle and Berwick Company brought about the ruin of Hudson's reputation.

By wholesale juggling of the capital and revenue accounts, and by adjustment of the finances of the two northern companies of which he was Chairman (the York and North Midland, and the York, Newcastle and Berwick), the shareholders of both had been presented with a largely false statement as to the actual state of affairs, and the dividends paid were far higher than circumstances warranted. There was a deal in rails that turned out of immense profit to Mr. Hudson himself, and he had a way of appropriating surplus shares, distributing some to friends and taking the remainder as his own personal property. He certainly rendered great services to the companies, but in rewarding himself thus he acted without sanction, and indeed without knowledge of his fellow directors.

Perhaps the most astounding instance was his taking for his own use no less than 10,894 Newcastle & Berwick shares, but signing for them on behalf of the company! Revelation of dealings such as this by a man who had enjoyed the absolute confidence of railway investors had a catastrophic effect upon the railway share market. It is a saddening reflection that one to whom Mr. Gladstone later referred as "a man of great discernment, possessing a great deal of courage and rich enterprise . . ." ". . . a very bold, and not at all an unwise projector" could have so disregarded the ethics of business as to indulge in such practices.

Hudson was a financier with apparently very little knowledge of railway operation. One can understand up to a point his jeers at those sponsoring the rival line to the north; "These juvenile promoters" he prophesied "would have spent every shilling of their capital by the time they had arrived at Grantham . . . if it were united with that humbug, the Atmospheric, the London and York would be the most complete thing in the world". But as the menace to his interests grew so his language became more reckless, and at the Midland meeting in 1845 he said: "I challenge them to leave London with twenty coaches and I will beat them to York, and what is more I don't believe they will get there at all on a thick foggy day when the rails are greasy."

After this meeting Hudson met Edmund Dennison, the Chairman-to-be of the London and York, on Derby station platform, and told him bluntly that they would never have got enough money to get to Grantham if they had got it honestly!

Dennison thereupon called Hudson a blackguard to his face, and turned his back on him.

Hudson realising he had perhaps gone too far tried to explain it away, but Dennison was inflexible: "Hudson," he said, "I've done with you; go away!"

The subsequent activities of the Midland Railway make up a story that is in many ways typical of the general scramble that took place in Mid-Victorian years. It was repeated, on a lesser scale, in a score of districts, and led to the establishment of a number of highly competitive routes. By the opening of the Great Northern Railway the Midland was deprived of its importance as a link in the route from London to the North-East, though still serving Leeds. But the ambition of the Midland Board knew no bounds and they determined upon a policy of expansion that eventually took their tracks to the Scottish border, to the Bristol Channel, to London, and finally to Shoeburyness. When the London extension was planned they were clearly feeling their way. The line was built first from Leicester to Hitchin, from which latter junction they obtained running powers over the Great Northern Railway to King's Cross.

When the traffic was being built up this arrangement worked well enough, but eventually the congestion grew; the Great Northern, as owners, naturally gave their own trains priority and the Midland traffic situation between Hitchin and King's Cross became little short of chaotic. Protests were made, which of course the Great Northern swept aside. Disputes became more and more frequent until matters culminated in one of those high-handed actions that characterised dealings between the different companies in early days. On the last day of June 1862 the Great Northern evicted or rather attempted to evict the Midland from the sidings at King's Cross! The resulting confusion was simply indescribable. It was of course necessary to patch up an agreement, but this was only a temporary measure pending the construction of the Midland Railway's own line to London, which was completed in 1868.

While Hudson was pushing ahead with his scheme for the completion of the East Coast route into Scotland his activities were viewed with some concern by the Grand Junction. Hitherto this latter company, and their ally the London and Birmingham, had enjoyed a monopoly of the Anglo-Scottish traffic, through their northward connexion with the Preston and Wyre Railway. The terminus of the line was at Fleetwood, whence passengers took steamer to Ardrossan, and completed their journey over the tracks of the Glasgow, Kilmarnock and Ayr Railway. That was in 1841. But the activities of Hudson and his friends led the Grand Junction to make prompt retaliation, and they instructed their engineer, Joseph Locke, to survey the country between Preston and Carlisle with a view to making a railway to the Scottish border.

The terrain was infinitely more difficult than that traversed by the East Coast route; the Pennines, the Westmorland Fell Country and the Lakeland mountains were ranged athwart the direct line, while the deeply indented coastline of North Lancashire and Cumberland presented many obstacles to any proposed low-level route. As early as 1836 George Stephenson had been consulted as to the practicability of a West Coast route to Scotland, and he, doubtless with the idea of preserving easy gradients, suggested that the line would have to cross part of Morecambe Bay and then proceed up the coast. As a trunk route this would have been too roundabout;

the actual distance from Lancaster to Whitehaven by rail today is 80½ miles, whereas it is only 49 miles as the crow flies. Add to this another 40 miles from Whitehaven to Carlisle, and this route totals 120½ miles, against less than 70 in a straight line.

By the time Locke came to survey the course in real earnest much of the old prejudice against heavy gradients had vanished. In any event it was a case of "Hobson's Choice" in the country through which the Lancaster and Carlisle must pass; for unless the line was to wind a sinuous way through the Lake District and pass over Dunmail Raise at an altitude of 728 ft. above sea level the only alternative was to cross the water-shed between the head waters of the Lune and the Lowther, in the gap between the heights of Crosby Ravensworth moor and the Shap Fells. The altitude here is 915 ft. and it lies only 30 miles north of Morecambe Bay. Locke decided early upon the Shap route, and somewhat naturally proposed to carry the line up the Lune valley throughout from Lancaster, where the gradients would in no place be steeper than 1 in 147.

On the other hand the district traversed was sparsely populated—Kirkby Lonsdale being the only place of any size; whereas, to the west lay the important town of Kendal. Local interests called for the survey of this alternative route. It involved heavier grading with a maximum steepness of 1 in 106; but the claims of Kendal outweighed this operational drawback, and the more westerly route was finally agreed upon. And so the West Coast trains of today have the formidable Grayrigg Bank to surmount—13 miles of really hard going—until,

52

on a brief falling gradient, they sweep round the curve into the Lune Gorge, at Low Gill. For those who enjoy wild country the line almost from the moment of leaving the shores of Morecambe Bay is one of the scenic gems of the English railways.

Above Kendal the track is carried high on a shoulder of Hay Fell, and presents a magnificent prospect westwards to the Lakeland mountains, where many famous summits can be picked out on a clear day. Pounding on, up a gradient of 1 in 106, among age-old hills that crowd closer and closer upon the railway, one can truly sense something of the profound solitude and grandeur of the fell country. At high speed this vivid impression would be lost, but at 35 to 40 m.p.h. there is time to hear the noise of the rushing mountain streams that pass under the railway; the panorama unfolds and enfolds with a slow deliberation, and all the time the heavy exhaust beat of the locomotive comes as a reminder that we are climbing steeply.

The gorge of the Lune ends about two miles south of Orton village, and the country to the north rises steeply to the watershed. With a view to keeping the gradient down as much as possible Locke first proposed to tunnel under the ridge. As constructed however the line was carried over the open moorland, with no heavier works than a deep, though relatively short cutting near the summit; the result was an incline that has been the bugbear of the locomotive department ever since. It was singularly appropriate that the first sod turned in the building of the Lancaster and Carlisle Railway should have been on this incline, for "Shap", with its 4 miles of

1 in 75 ascent, has proved the dominating physical feature, not only of the mountain section but of the entire route from London to Carlisle.

Successive generations of Crewe-built locomotives were able to keep good time with the heaviest Scottish expresses till they came to the north end of the Lune gorge; but then their enginemen were often glad to take assistance up to Shap Summit. The hamlet of Tebay, where a junction was later made with the North-Eastern line running across country to Darlington, became an important banking station, where powerful engines were kept in steam to provide rear end assistance to passenger and freight trains. Beyond Shap, the scenery on the run down to Carlisle is relatively quiet by comparison with the majestic scenes passed on the way to the summit, though there is one brief, though glorious prospect eastward to the Pennines while the train is racing over Clifton Moor.

The Lancaster and Carlisle Railway was opened to traffic in December 1846, but shortly before this its two chief sponsors, the London and Birmingham, and the Grand Junction, had amalgamated, and taken the name that was destined to become world famous as that of the premier line of Great Britain—the London and North Western Railway. The working of the Lancaster and Carlisle was taken over by the L.N.W.R. in 1859 on a 999-year lease, and one clause of this agreement sounds a somewhat humorous note today. It was specified that "the plant, rolling stock and movable property to be used by the lessees during, and to be restored at the end of, the lease". The lawyers who drew up that agreement must have had a very sanguine view of the staying power of the old L. & C. locomotives!

Carlisle was not the ultimate goal of Grand Junction ambitions when Joseph Locke was first instructed to survey the country north of Preston. Glasgow was the real goal, and as early as 1835 Locke was prospecting to right and left of Telford's coach road up Annandale. This enterprising action of the Grand Junction Railway was not received with favour in Scotland.

A rival project fostered in Glasgow favoured a route of easier grading up Nithsdale, and Locke himself considered the Annandale scheme to be impracticable owing to the severity of the incline that would be unavoidable north of Beattock. But two prominent landed proprietors, J. J. Hope Johnstone and Charles Stewart, brought such pressure to bear that the rival schemes were eventually submitted to examination by a Government Commission.

It was largely at Locke's suggestion that this Commission was set up, but the fact that the Government of Sir Robert Peel did intervene is a matter of no mean significance. In a speech in the House of Commons in 1888 Gladstone recalled the circumstances. " . . . the House may be curious to know why it was the Government did so, when, I believe, there is no other example in the entire history of railways of their having attempted anything of the kind. I remember perfectly well the motive of the Government. The motive was that, as it was known, or firmly believed, to be absolutely impossible that there should ever be more than one railway into Scotland (laughter)—it was considered of the highest importance that the best scientific power of the country should be brought to bear on the choice of the line (renewed laughter)."

Despite the forebodings of Locke the choice fell upon the Annandale route. Thus was born the line which, despite its English origin, eventually presented a wholly Scottish façade with the picturesque name of the Caledonian Railway. Construction began in 1845, but the idea of having only one railway from England into Scotland did not last for long, and the Glaswegians went ahead with their own long-cherished scheme for a line to the south, through Kilmarnock, the Burns country, and down Nithsdale. So the Glasgow and South Western Railway came into being—from the very outset a deadly rival of the Caledonian.

Even now, after the two companies have for nearly forty years been together merged first in the L.M.S and now in Scottish Region, men of the old "Sou-West" still speak in scornful terms of the Caley, a sentiment that would be flung back in their teeth from many quiet corners of the Annandale route. However, more of this later. At the moment we are concerned with the building up of the British railway system. In Scotland it certainly went ahead with great vigour once the Caledonian Railway was authorised, and by April 1850 the line itself was not only complete, but by further railways, which were later absorbed by the Caledonian, the tracks had been carried to Aberdeen, and through railway communication between London and the "Granite City" established. For the whole of this great Scottish system, extending from Carlisle to Aberdeen, and connecting the west and east coast shipping ports in one network, Joseph Locke was the engineer.

But even before this, railway fever had penetrated the Highland fastnesses. The circumstances were however very different from those animating George Hudson and his associates, or the men of the Grand Junction who sent Locke into Scotland. Among the Highland Chieftains, and men of business or influence in Inverness and the Far North, there had been growing anxiety at the steady depopulating of the whole Highland region. The breaking down of the Clan System after the second Jacobite rebellion rendered destitute a large proportion of a once-thriving community, and the men sought employment in the cities of the Lowlands, or overseas. A group of prominent Highlanders saw in the railway an opportunity for a revival of trade, a chance to bring back the people to the country they had so unwillingly left.

In 1845, just when the Railway Mania was beginning to gain momentum, a scheme was put forward for a railway from Inverness to Perth. This bold proposal emanated wholly from Inverness, and the promoters enlisted the services of a fellow-townsman, Joseph Mitchell, as engineer. One of the ablest men of his profession, Mitchell proposed a route closely following that of the stage coaches, crossing the Monadhliath mountains at an altitude of 1,323 ft.,* and the Grampians through the Pass of Druimuachdar, at 1,462 ft.* above sea level. The Parliamentary Committee turned down this proposal as impracticable. One of the opposing counsel is reported to have made merry at Mitchell's expense, thus: "Ascend-

* The summit levels as actually built are 1,315 and 1,484 ft.

ing such a summit as 1,450 ft. was very unprecedented, and Mr. Mitchell, the engineer, was the greatest mountain climber he had heard of. He beat Napoleon outright, and quite eclipsed Hannibal. He read a book the other day, of several hundred pages, describing how Hannibal crossed the Alps, but after this line had been passed he had no doubt quartos would be written about Mr. Mitchell!" The opposition seemed to have made much capital out of the high altitudes proposed for the Inverness—Perth line. It is typical of the contradictions abroad during this early railway period that just about this time Parliament was giving preference to the Annandale, instead of the Nithsdale route from Carlisle to Glasgow, even though the former included gradients almost as steep and not much shorter than those proposed in the Highlands, and attained an altitude of 1,014 ft. at Beattock Summit against the 616 ft. of the rival route!

So it was not until ten years later that the first link in the railway to the south was built from Inverness, and then only a level track along the shore of the Moray Firth, to Nairn; the mountain route to link up with the Perth and Dunkeld railway was not authorised until 1861. It is indeed extraordinary, in view of the general economic conditions prevailing in the Highlands at the time, that the whole of this great enterprise should have been financed locally, and in many cases with an almost complete disregard of the prospects of getting an early return upon investments. On many occasions the Highland Railway was literally dependent upon the generosity of directors and shareholders for the very continuance of its operation. In a gallant story many famous Highland names, names more usually associated with the stormy days of the Jacobite rebellions and clan warfare, feature in a new guise: Cluny Macpherson; Mackintosh of Raigmore; the Earl of Seafield (chief of the Clan Grant); the Marquis of Breadalbane; Macleod of Cadboll; and the Duke of Atholl. Behind them was the skill and resource of Joseph Mitchell, the engineer, who built this great trunk line largely along the route proposed in 1845, and so gave us one of the grandest pieces of railway in all Britain.

Like many lovers of Scotland I had often made the railway journey to Inverness in early autumn, and had enjoyed the beauty of hills glowing purple with heather, the first changing tints in the forests, and the ever-fascinating succession of straths, open moorlands, pine-fringed lochans and broad mountain vistas. But still I was mainly ignorant of the true spirit of the Highland Railway, and of the sublime grandeur of the country through which it passes. Then one January night I had occasion to travel by the Royal Highlander, the sleeping-car express leaving Euston at 7.30 p.m. From Perth I rode on the engine. The winter's dawn broke serene and cloudless, and with snow lying deep we forged our way uphill through the usually grim and inhospitable Glen Garry into a world of hills dazzling white in the early sunshine. But the moment we breasted the summit of the Druimuachdar Pass the weather changed. We ran through squall after squall of driving sleet and snow; ice packed up against the cab glasses, and visibility was just about nil at times. The weather was clear at Aviemore while we changed engines, but again it was in a veritable blizzard, with snow driving clean through the cab, that we thundered up among the Monadhliath mountains to reach the pass of Slochd Mhuic. It was a real Highland occasion. My enginemen hosts were not only highland in speech but in name—Nicholson, Robertson, McLeod, Wilson, Monro and Malcolm— and I had the privilege of seeing them at work under the toughest of conditions.

The prospects of remunerative business were bleaker still when the opening up of the West Highlands came to be undertaken. It was not until 1865 that the first step in this direction was made, with the authorisation of the Callander and Oban Railway; but many were the vicissitudes of fortune experienced before the railway system of the West Highlands was completed. Here was no opportunity for building on the lavish scale of a Stephenson or a Brunel. Everything had to be built as cheaply as possible; the viaducts were of comparatively light construction; lengthy detours were made in order to avoid heavy earthworks, indeed so much do these routes follow the lie of the land that it is difficult to detect their courses when scanning the hillsides up which they make a winding way.

In spite of this, construction work on the Callander and Oban Railway was twice stopped through lack of funds. Whereas the great pioneers who built the London and Birmingham, the Great Western, and other early railways were handicapped by the primitive nature of the tools at their disposal railway builders in the West Highlands experienced some of their greatest difficulties in the almost total lack of transport facilities for their materials. The roads, where any existed, were in an appalling condition, and in many cases materials and stores had to be carried across trackless moorlands by pack-horses. In the year of grace 1897, when work was commenced on the Mallaig extension line, the contractors conveyed their materials by boat, establishing various bases along the shores of Loch Eil. This line, built particularly to serve the agriculture and fisheries of the Outer Isles, was subsidised by the Government, which guaranteed for thirty years a dividend of 3 per cent per annum upon £260,000; this latter figure was roughly half the capital cost of the railway.

The Highland Railway branch westward from Dingwall, which terminated first at Strome Ferry and was in 1897 extended to the Kyle of Lochalsh, provides a service complementary to that of the West Highland, running from Helensburgh, on the Firth of Clyde, to Fort William and thence to Mallaig. On all these routes the incessant curvature of the track and the steepness of the gradients impose a moderate speed of travel that gives ample opportunity for the majestic scenery to be enjoyed to the full. There is the terrific pull out of Balquhidder, on the Oban line, where the train pounds at 20 m.p.h. up the hillside overlooking Loch Earn; and then thunders on into the wild and narrowing morain of Glen Ogle: the descent of Glen Carron, on the Lochalsh line, to the widening valley and the sea-loch Carron; on to the narrows at Strome Ferry, and then to that thrilling first glimpse of the hills of Skye.

The West Highland line has many breathtaking scenes —the great volcano-like peak of Beinn Dorain, the wilderness of Rannoch Moor, and the dramatic succession of mountains and sea lochs on the Mallaig extension; but the scene that is, perhaps, of the most startling beauty comes almost at the outset of the run northwards from Helensburgh, where at the tiny station of Whistlefield the railway comes out on to the edge of a steep hillside; far below is Loch Long, winding sinuously among the mountains, and right opposite is the entrance to a still narrower fjord, Loch Goil. The very suddenness of its appearance makes this scene leave a most vivid impression, whether it be on a still summer day when the hills are mirrored in the loch, or in early spring when the highest peaks are still snow-clad and the water is the colour of steel.

In the latter half of the Victorian era the forging of some of the last links in the British railway network brought episodes as dramatic as any in this story: the driving of the Midland line from Settle through some of the wildest regions of the Pennines to reach Carlisle; the epic of the Severn Tunnel; the crossing of the Firths of Forth and Tay, where a tragic story of human frailty and the inevitable disaster that followed proved merely a prologue to the greatest triumph of British railway engineering.

Even as late as the year 1870, with all the early experience of railway building available, the construction of the Settle and Carlisle was a work of the first magnitude. Frederick Williams, writing in 1877, aptly summarises the task of the engineers: "It was well known, when the Midland Company decided to secure a route of their own to the gates of Scotland, that no common difficulties would have to be overcome. Years before, Mr. Locke, the eminent engineer, had been daunted by the obstacles he met, and had declared that even a west coast route to Scotland was impossible. . . . Across the whole North of England lay too the giant Pennine Chain, which seemed resolved to bar the way against any further access for an innovating and obtrusive civilization.

"Undaunted, however, by these obstacles, the General Manager and the Engineer-in-Chief of the Midland Company went down to see for themselves what could be done. In their researches they ascertained that there was one, the only one, practicable route. The great wolds and hills that stretch far over the West Riding of Yorkshire are fortunately bounded by one series of natural valleys that run from south to north, flanking the western outlines of the county, continuing across Westmorland, and forming part of the great Eden Valley of Cumberland. But when we speak of a series of valleys, we must not be misunderstood. It was no easy thing to find a route for a railway even among these. Over any such path frowned the huge masses of Ingleborough, and Whernside, and Wildboar, and Shap Fells; and if a line were to wind its way at the feet of these, and up and down those mighty dales, it would have to be by spanning valleys with stupendous viaducts, and piercing mountain-heights with enormous tunnels; miles upon miles of cuttings would have to be blasted through the rock, or literally torn through clay of the most extraordinary tenacity; and embankments, weighing perhaps 250,000 tons, would have to be piled on peaty moors, on some parts of which a horse could not walk without sinking up to his belly."

My own boyhood was spent in that rugged country-side. Mighty dales! How vividly the words portray the whole life and spirit of that region. How faithfully too those same words depict the scene that bursts upon a northbound traveller when his train emerges from the Blea Moor tunnel, and a few seconds later skims across the 100 ft.-high arches of Dent Head viaduct. On a route so packed with scenes of mountain splendour there is a great temptation, especially to an author with many personal memories, to linger in the district and dwell one by one upon the successive feats of engineering by which the dales were bridged, and the mountain flanks were tunnelled. Space, however, precludes any such lingerings!

Despite the natural obstacles the road is a magnificent one. The gradient is nowhere steeper than 1 in 100, although to be sure there are many miles so inclined; but more important still, the alignment is so good that not a single speed restriction is regularly enforced in the whole 70 miles of mountain railway. Today, the Anglo-Scottish expresses, after forging their way up hill at 40 to 45 m.p.h., go sweeping down through the dales at 80, 85 and sometimes over 90 m.p.h. For ten miles the line makes an almost level track at about 1,100 feet above sea level, and it is in this section, between Blea Moor and the summit at Ais Ghyll, that the scenery is at its wildest. It can be bleak and forbidding enough at times, and the snow fences on the cutting sides near Dent tell their own tale.

Ever since constructional days the Settle and Carlisle has been the scene of great and moving railway events. After the grouping in 1923 it was the arena to which the crack locomotives of each constituent company of the L.M.S were sent, to be tested one against the other; Caledonian, and London and North Western engines, manned by their own crews, came here to be tested against the Midland locomotives, and so keen grew this friendly competition that it is no exaggeration to say the loads eventually taken over Aisgill summit astonished even the highest locomotive authorities. In the last sentence I have quoted the somewhat prosaic railway spelling of that euphonious Yorkshire name. It is one of the bleakest spots on the route, under the lowering flanks of Wild Boar Fell. A place of poignant memories, too, where twice in one decade the night sky glowed ominously red from a burning sleeping car express—victims of two of the saddest accidents in our railway history.

The river Severn, like the estuaries of the Forth and Tay, in Scotland, presented a natural barrier to the building of a direct line of railway between important centres of industry. Brunel carried the main line to South Wales through Gloucester, and this line was opened to Swansea in 1850; but the earliest railway communication between Bristol and South Wales involved the use of a ferry, which was inaugurated specially for handling traffic of the Bristol and South Wales Union Railway. This "New Passage" ferry crossed the Severn at a point some four miles below the "Old Passage" ferry, from Aust to Beachley, near Chepstow. But even before the new ferry was in operation engineers of the day were already thinking of some speedier means of transit.

Charles Richardson, while building the "New Passage" ferry piers, conceived the idea of a tunnel under the river, though it was not until the Great Western took up the scheme that the sanction of Parliament was obtained. In face of all the known difficulties it was a tremendous undertaking to drive a tunnel $4\frac{1}{4}$ miles long under a tidal estuary. But the task proved infinitely more hazardous than was expected. The river is over two miles wide at the site of the New Passage ferry, and it was adjacent to this line that the tunnel was planned. At the outset the greatest risk appeared to be in tunnelling beneath the Shoots, a deep channel 1,200 feet wide, where the water is 95 feet deep at high water, and through which the ebbing tide flows at no less than 10 knots. The lowest point of the tunnel is beneath the Shoots and here there is a depth of 45 feet between river bottom and the top of the tunnel. To obtain this depth the railway descends on a gradient of 1 in 100 from the Gloucestershire side, and ascends at 1 in 90 on the other.

Work was commenced in 1873, with Richardson in charge locally, and Sir John Hawkshaw acting as Consulting Engineer. Progress was very slow at first, and after four and a half years all that had been accomplished was to sink one shaft on the Welsh bank of the river and from this to drive a drainage heading under the Shoots, a distance of 1,600 yards. The Great Western Railway then divided the work, as originally planned, into sections and various additional contracts were let; but in 1879 the whole of the workings on the Welsh side were flooded when a fresh-water spring was tapped. The story of the next two years is one of continual struggle against the flood water. Powerful pumping machinery was installed, but the whole works seemed dogged with misfortune.

Dams were built to keep out the Big Spring, as it was called; but the water burst in elsewhere. One of the pumps suddenly broke to pieces. Workmen's cottages near the river banks were flooded by a tidal wave, and vast quantities of timber were washed away. At the same time the fires of the pumping engines were extinguished, and a great volume of water poured down one of the shafts to increase the flooding below. On a later occasion, a sudden burst near a headwall sent another cataract plunging down the shaft, and trapped a number of men working in the tunnel; to rescue them a boat had to be lowered down the shaft.

Among such a succession of unexpected and alarming occurrences one can only think with reverence of the engineers who with such resolution kept things going, and of the men who worked for so many years below ground in constant danger and dire discomfort. Among the men the heroism of Diver Lambert was outstanding. When the Big Spring irrupted a door in the headwall had been left open. In face of the flood water the workings had been hurriedly abandoned, and tools and materials were left where they lay. To assist in clearing the water it was necessary to close that door in the headwall, and Lambert made his way for over 300 yards along this dark flooded passage, past numerous obstacles and debris. After three attempts this brave man succeeded. In the winter of 1881 an exceptionally heavy snowstorm held up deliveries of coal for the pumping engines for three days, and the severe frost stopped all work above ground for a fortnight.

More and more pumps were installed, and the waters of the Big Spring diverted away from the tunnel. Gradually the troubles were overcome, and in 1885 the work was completed. It was, however, not until the late autumn of 1886 that regular traffic was worked through the tunnel. Though saving 25 miles on the journey between London and South Wales it remains a work requiring constant vigilance. In 1929 train crews reported that water was falling in certain places; examination revealed that jets of water as big as a man's fist were flying horizontally from one side of the tunnel to the other. Above the roof at this particular point there happened to be 45 to 50 feet of solid rock, and the trouble appeared to have arisen from the development of a fissure in the rock. At high tide there was 15 ft. of water, and a careful search at last discovered a small whirlpool; at low tide the rocks were uncovered and a large fissure was duly revealed. It was filled with cement, in bags, and a large area surrounding the spot was also covered with cement concrete. By this means, carried out entirely between tides, the fissure was sealed off.

The steep gradients leading down under the river make very difficult the operation of heavy trains. Fortunately the line is straight almost throughout, and with a clear road the expresses can go full tilt down one side and rush the other; on one occasion indeed an express from London to Cardiff attained a speed of 98 m.p.h. under the river! But the heavy coal trains from South Wales require to be double-headed, and their slow passage makes the tunnel section a definite bottleneck. The alternative of a bridge never appears to have been considered in the prospecting days, though if the present scheme for harnessing the tremendous tidal power of the Severn ever comes to fruition the barrage will most likely be built to include a road and railway bridge, both of which would be of incalculable value.

Railway communication between Edinburgh and Dundee, across the estuaries of the Forth and Tay was established in 1848; but it was a very slow business, by ferry from Granton to Burntisland and again from Tayport to Broughty Ferry Pier. Nevertheless the service was considered a fine achievement at the time, and brought great credit upon Thomas Bouch, who was generally considered responsible. Actually the credit was wrongly bestowed, though Bouch profited from it to the extent of being appointed Manager of the Edinburgh, Perth and Dundee Railway in 1849. A fateful association was thus established. He seems to have been a man quite apart from the usual characters of early railway engineers; a man of boundless ambition, one who was associated with countless projects, yet taking little real responsibility in their execution. The Belah Viaduct for example, on the line from Darlington to Penrith, is credited to him, though the entire design was due to Mr. Robert H. Bow.

Bouch, by his somewhat unorthodox methods, built up a great reputation, and when the North British Railway obtained Parliamentary sanction to build both the Forth and the Tay bridges he was appointed engineer for the entire work. As a bridge designer he was probably no less mathematical than others of his day, but while they advanced cautiously his methods can only be described as reckless. In one case, the lofty viaduct over Hownes Gill near Consett, County Durham, the railway company consulted Robert Stephenson before accepting Bouch's design; it was a most artistic creation, but Stephenson altered it considerably, buttressing the piers and generally increasing its strength. In spite of occasional incidents of this kind Bouch's reputation was further enhanced and his design for the Tay Bridge was hailed as one of the greatest of the day.

In actual fact it was a disgrace to British engineering, both in the casualness of its design and the shoddy workmanship put into its construction. In design Bouch seemed to have paid little heed to the significant alterations Robert Stephenson made to the Hownes Gill viaduct. The first Tay Bridge has been aptly described as a bridge built on stilts, and weak stilts at that. In general conception it was frail, with little lateral stability to withstand the gales which frequently swept in from the North Sea. In detail design it was fundamentally unsound. Of the methods used in its construction the less said the better. Bouch may be pardoned for his ignorance of the effects of wind pressure, but he cannot be exonerated for his negligence, as revealed in the general lack of supervision during the constructional work. As a result, to his bad design were added some atrocious makeshifts in building.

The bridge was duly completed, and, after what must have been a somewhat cursory examination by the Board of Trade, was opened to traffic in May 1878. Just over a year later Queen Victoria travelled over it on her way to Balmoral, and shortly afterwards she knighted Thomas Bouch. With his reputation soaring to its zenith he proceeded with a scheme for a colossal suspension bridge over the Firth of Forth, and then came the absolutely inevitable tragedy. On the night of December 28th, 1879 a great storm was raging on the east coast of Scotland, and at the height of this storm the 5.27 p.m. mail train from Burntisland to Dundee entered upon the Tay Bridge; it reached the high girders over the navigable part of the firth, and then this entire central portion of the bridge collapsed, taking with it the train. Every one of the eighty persons on board perished. The marvel was that so weak and flimsy a structure lasted as long as it did.

The disaster to the first Tay Bridge had one good result: it prevented Bouch from committing an even greater folly. His Tay Bridge was bad enough, poorly conceived, and designed with flagrant violations of engineering fundamentals; but his scheme for crossing the Firth of Forth was a fantastic conception. The site of his proposed bridge was alongside the Queensferry passage, where the islet of Inchgarvie in mid-stream provided an ideal base for a central pier. At low tide the firth is about 4,000 feet wide at this point, and from a central tower Bouch's scheme consisted of two enormous spans of about 1,600 feet over the navigable waterway on either side of Inchgarvie. When it is recalled that for carrying railways the largest spans in the country at that time were those of the Britannia tubular bridge, 460 feet, closely followed by the 455 feet spans of Brunel's great viaduct at Saltash, the daring nature of Bouch's proposals will be better appreciated. And it was to be a suspension bridge too! As designed the towers were to have been 550 feet high. Although the sanction of Parliament was obtained, for some reason—it may have been a feeling of uncertainty, or on the other hand a mere formality—Sir John Hawkshaw was asked to report on the design. He found it satisfactory in all respects *provided it was assumed that the pressure exerted by an extreme gale of wind did not exceed 10 pounds per square foot.* The italics are mine.

In the light of subsequent events this report may be taken as non-committal, but at the time it was accepted as an affirmative. The contracts were let, and work was begun. Then came the disaster to the Tay Bridge. Naturally public confidence in Bouch was shattered; his design for the Forth Bridge was examined in a much more critical light, and the scheme abandoned as unsound. It was perhaps typical of Bouch and his kind, that when catastrophe came he strove to place all the blame on others. The subsequent enquiry certainly brought to light the sketchy data existing at that time on the subject of wind pressure. One of Bouch's assistants had to rely on some figures presented to the Royal Society in 1759 by Smeaton, and when, in 1873, the Astronomer Royal, Sir George Airy, was consulted as to the likely pressures to be experienced on Bouch's Forth Bridge, he quoted the same figure, namely, 10 pounds per square foot. During the course of the enquiry into the Tay Bridge disaster Sir George Airy was called as an expert witness, and he then asserted that a pressure of 120 pounds per square foot should have been allowed for! That was in 1880, only seven years after his previous recommendation.

Today Bouch's proposal for crossing the Firth of Forth is vividly recalled by the gigantic towers of the new road bridge so near to the railway bridge of 1890; for this new structure is to be a suspension bridge. By this I do not wish to cause any apprehension, for modern road traffic, heavy though it is, is not to be compared with the conveyance of an express train of 700 tons, in one unit.

It was significant of the general apprehension over the effects of wind pressure, following the collapse of the Tay Bridge, that a lofty viaduct near Staithes, on the coastal railway from Saltburn to Whitby, then unfinished, was greatly strengthened before trains were permitted to run over it. This viaduct has an unusual safety device attached to it—a wind pressure gauge—which causes an electric bell to ring in Staithes signal box when the pressure of the wind is such as to make it unsafe for trains to cross. This apparatus was installed in 1884, shortly after the opening of the railway, but since that time the bell has been rung on only a very few occasions. After gales causing wind pressure high enough to ring the bell the viaduct is inspected by bridge engineers before trains are permitted to cross.

For a little time after Bouch's scheme was abandoned the proposal for a bridge over the Firth of Forth hung fire. Then in 1882 the matter was referred to a firm of consulting engineers, Messrs. Barlow, Harrison and Fowler. The onus of the work was shouldered by John Fowler, and his brilliant assistant Benjamin Baker. It was not merely a question of engineering skill. The spectre of the first Tay Bridge was present in every engineer's mind, yet Fowler and Baker set out with supreme courage to build what is still one of the greatest and most wonderful bridges in the world. With them must be associated the name of the contractor, William Arrol.

Although the principle they worked upon as applied to a huge modern railway bridge was entirely new, Baker drew attention to its ancient origin. Skeleton bridges embodying the same general idea have been found in various parts of the world and thought to be the work of early men, and of these a particular example, in Tibet, has been referred to by Baker as a faint prototype of the Forth Bridge. This principle is that of the cantilever; a girder supported only at the centre, yet strong enough to carry its own weight and any loads which may be applied, whether at the centre, the extreme ends, or anywhere else. The Forth Bridge consists of three cantilever girders, of such beauty and of such elegant proportions that the magnitude of the structure as a whole and the massive nature of its details are never obtrusive. It took $6\frac{1}{2}$ years to construct, and was opened on March 4th 1890, by H.R.H. the Prince of Wales, later King Edward VII. The new Tay Bridge was designed by W. H. Barlow, of the same firm of consulting engineers, and constructed by William Arrol. A massive, though undistinguished structure, it was opened for traffic in 1887.

In the course of travelling to Aberdeen and beyond I have many times crossed the Forth Bridge, but one particular journey stands out in my memory. It was at night on the southbound Aberdonian sleeping car express, and

I was riding in the cab of Sir Nigel Gresley's big 2–8–2 engine *Cock O' the North*. With an enormous trainload the performance throughout from Dundee had been a veritable classic, but as we forged our way up the 1 in 70 gradient towards the bridge every single feature which had gone to make up the thrill and exhilaration of the trip seemed to work up to a tremendous climax. On the footplate the atmosphere was thick with flying coal dust; the smell of hot oil mixed strangely with gusts of keen night air. In Queensferry tunnel *Cock O' the North* literally roared, while little stabs of flame shot from the chimney, hit the roof, and rebounded in a shower over the cab. At a steady 19 m.p.h. we came out into the open, and so on to the Forth Bridge. Crossing on the footplate is an unforgettable experience, especially at night: a deep hollow reverberation from our wheels; each cross girder lit up by the glare of the fire as we passed underneath; far below, the mast lights of ships; and all the time *Cock O' the North*'s sharp staccato beat rising high above all.

Our load that night was a testimony to the foresight of the designers of the Forth Bridge. The locomotive used at the opening ceremony in 1890 weighed 46 tons, and an Aberdeen express with its engine and tender did not usually scale much more than 200 tons. On that summer night in 1935 when I was on the "Aberdonian" our engine and train together weighed just seven hundred tons!

3

Their Working and Equipment

THE ROAD

"THE story to be told is one of magnificent and continuing achievement, for progress has been steady, and the last few years have demonstrated that the railway, as a means of land transport, is still unsurpassed. Instead of having passed its zenith, it has not yet reached it, and it is upon the solid foundation and the excellence of its permanent way that the whole structure stands, both firm and secure."

Thus wrote Mr. C. E. R. Sherrington in a souvenir booklet celebrating the Diamond Jubilee of the Permanent Way Institution. For many years British track was peculiar, when compared with that of railways in other parts of the world, in its use of a bull-head rail resting and keyed in cast iron chairs; elsewhere the almost universal practice is to use flat-bottomed rails spiked to the sleepers, either direct or with a steel bearing plate between. The use of bull-head, or double-headed rails in this country can be traced back to 1834, when an early form was in use on the Bodmin and Wadebridge Railway.

But the invention which had by far the greatest influence upon the subsequent form of British permanent way was due to Joseph Locke. In 1835 he designed and put into service some double-headed rails in which both heads were the same size. His intention was to make these rails serve a double term of duty, for when one head was worn down with the constant passage of traffic the rail would be turned upside down and the other head used. In actual practice it was found that the under head became so battered where it rested on the chairs that it was unfit for any service after turning. But although the double-headed rail did not fill the function for which it was originally designed the chaired road proved so much more satisfactory than the American and Continental tracks laid with flat-bottomed rails spiked direct to the sleepers that it became thoroughly established as the standard form of British permanent way. It is only recently under the burden of heavier loads and still higher speeds that its supremacy in British traffic conditions has been questioned.

Following a series of trials made just before national-ization, on the Great Western, the London Midland and Scottish, and on the London and North Eastern Rail-ways the British Transport Commission decided to change to flat-bottomed rails for the future British standard track. The trials were, in the first place, a general seeking after a stiffer road that will carry modern high speed trains without excessive maintenance. A flat-bottomed rail itself has a greater lateral stiffness than a bull-head rail of equal weight; but that is not all. The broad base of British rail chairs adds greatly to the general stiffness of the road, while at the same time American fastenings have in recent years become a great deal more elaborate than the direct spiking of earlier days.

Purely on sentimental grounds this epoch-making change in the form of our permanent way is much to be regretted. It had become so thoroughly established in lay minds as *the* British track, different from and superior to all others. An amusing instance of this occurred soon after the liberation of the Cherbourg peninsula in July 1944. Before D-day the daily newspapers had plentifully regaled us with stories of the vast supplies collected in Britain for the rehabilitation of the French railways, and in publishing a photograph of troops repairing a bombed station yard a lynx-eyed journalist of one paper had spotted bull-head rails and a chaired road. The attention of readers was drawn to this point, as evidence of the speed of reconstruction with British type of track. Unfortunately for his argument the rails held ready for service abroad were exclusively of the flat-bottomed type, since rapid relaying on existing sleepers would be necessary for military purposes. The explanation of the chaired road near Cherbourg is that the old Etat system which served Normandy and Brittany, was one of the very few railways outside Britain to use our form of track. One other is the Great Indian Peninsula Railway.

The term "permanent way" is in its strictest sense a misnomer, for the track is about the least permanent part of a railway! If left unattended the road would quickly lose its alignment, while on plain straight line the rails tend to move gradually in the direction of the traffic. This phenomenon, which is termed "rail creep", is believed to be due to the ironing-out effect of passing trains on track which has a certain amount of spring in it. The wooden-keys are slightly tapered, and to lessen

78

the amount of creep these keys are driven into the chairs in the direction of the traffic; thus any tendency of the rail to move forward will wedge them in more tightly. On sharp curves the outer rails move forward, and the inner sometimes shows a tendency to creep backwards.

The sleepers are held in position entirely by the ballast, and it is easy to appreciate how they may become pushed out of true alignment on a curve, due to the constant passage of traffic. Not only this: in places the rail level may sag out of true. Small variations in "top", as permanent way men term the rail level, are dealt with by packing additional ballast under the sleepers, but sometimes troubles of a more serious nature present themselves. Wet subsoils, particularly where the line is in a cutting, can prove a serious nuisance. Clay especially tends to become waterlogged and then to work up through the ballast; drainage is extremely difficult in such circumstances, and the road may become so unstable as to compel the imposition of a speed limit throughout the affected length. There was a case near Gretna in 1944 where maintenance was in progress, and the track consequently under observation; yet even so it was not apparent how dangerous the conditions were. In actual fact things were bad enough to cause the derailment, at 55 m.p.h., of a London to Glasgow sleeping car express.

Shortly before the war a very interesting operation was carried out on the Southern Railway main line between Sevenoaks and Tonbridge, where the line runs through a cutting in the Weald clay. So much trouble was experienced here, under heavy and fast traffic, that the novel procedure was adopted of inserting a mattress of pre-cast concrete slabs beneath the ballast. By their weight, which was augmented by laying a number of old rails on the top, these slabs have the effect of preventing any tendency for the clay to work up through the ballast. It is however one thing to conceive such a plan, but quite another to carry it out with the least possible interruption to traffic. There is nothing for it but to hand over the line to the engineers for certain periods, and to divert the traffic in the meantime. The Southern Railway was fortunate in having numerous alternative routes—the result of hectic competition for traffic in pre-amalgamation days. It was of course only at week-ends that such diversions could be arranged, and with "absolute possession" of the line limited to the period between 11 p.m. on Saturday nights and 3.45 a.m. on the following Monday mornings the work of strengthening the roadbeds had to be spread over eight week-ends. During these periods the work went forward day and night. The men worked in relays, and to ensure the utmost progress during the hours of darkness the cutting was brilliantly floodlit. During each of the week-ends, in lifting out old track, excavating, laying in the slabs and the new ballast, more than 1,000 tons of material had to be handled. Moreover, the whole site had to be cleared after the week-end's programme was complete, and the road left ready for the full weekday traffic to begin flowing on each Monday morning.

During the war we were occasionally given news of fine feats of repair work on the railways, in the Blitz and in the Flying Bomb attacks. Unstinted praise was

13 Railway owned docks: an aerial view of the very extensive installations at Cardiff, originally designed for the large-scale export of coal

14   The Irish Mail steamer "Cambria" at Holyhead

NOTABLE RAILWAY STEAMERS

15   The "Drive-on, drive-off" car carrier "Maid of Kent", on the Dover–
Boulogne car ferry service since 1959

16 London and North Western compound express locomotive "Queen Empress", painted in cream-white with scarlet and grey lining in celebration of the Diamond Jubilee of Queen Victoria, 1897

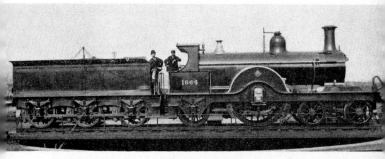

17 Midland Railway: A Johnson 4–2–2 single of 1889 vintage; 7 ft. 6 in. driving wheels

18 Caledonian Railway: "Dunalastair" class 4–4–0 of 1896

19 Among the high Pennines: St. Pancras to Edinburgh express crossing Arten Gill Viaduct near Dent, Yorkshire

20, One of Brunel's greatest works, the Royal Albert Bridge, Saltash, seen from the air alongside the recently opened Tamar suspension bridge

21 A modern station layout: the west end of Newcastle Central, showing the relatively few structures needed with modern colour light signals

22 Modern Freight Marshalling: a high level view of Temple Mills Yard, near Stratford, showing the wagon retarders, and the flood-lighting towers

23 Snow Plough unit, N.E. Region

24 A freight engine snowed-up on the Darlington–Tebay cross-country line near Barras

given to the organization the railways had developed for meeting such emergencies. The praise was richly deserved, but the organization behind such feats was no new thing. In 1932 the L.M.S Railway found it necessary to strengthen certain bridges over Millers Dale on the Derby-Manchester line, to permit of the running of heavier locomotives. Replacement of the existing girders one by one would have involved the imposition of a speed limit for a long period, and delay to traffic would have been considerable; accordingly a totally different method of renewal was adopted. The new superstructure, to be mounted on the old masonry piers, was erected complete on a specially built cradle abreast of the old bridge. Meanwhile traffic continued running at full speed until 1 a.m. on a certain Sunday morning; at that hour the engineers obtained "absolute possession". Then the permanent way was removed; the old girders were cut into portions by oxy-acetylene flame and lowered into the roadway and river below; finally the new bridge, weighing 650 tons, was rolled into position. The whole operation was completed by 8 a.m. the same morning— certainly a masterpiece of organization.

The gradual development of the South Wales Coalfield has had some curious, not to say alarming effects upon the railways in certain districts. In many places the underground workings are exceedingly complex; there are coal faces $2\frac{1}{2}$ miles distant from the shaft bottom, numerous very deep shafts, and often there are several worked-out seams one above the other. The cumulative effect of these workings is to cause subsidence of the ground on the surface. It would not be so bad if the sinking was uniform within a wide area; but owing to the varying number of worked-out seams beneath the ground some extraordinary phenomena have been observed, and the effect upon railway property has been serious. A case that was, perhaps, exceptional in its severity occurred at Trehafod in the Rhondda Valley, on the main line of the former Taff Vale Railway. Near the passenger station the ground has, over a number of years, sunk some 26ft. below its original level.

In this district the railway originally had a uniform gradient of 1 in 175 climbing up the valley, but the effect of the subsidence would have been to steepen the gradient locally to 1 in 21. This would have created such serious haulage difficulties that the track was lifted, to keep the gradient something nearer the original. But while the variations in level due to uneven subsidence can be largely corrected on embankments or in cuttings the problem is infinitely more complicated where viaducts are concerned. In the disturbed area at Trehafod the piers of a steel girder bridge sank unevenly and, although the track itself is periodically lifted and fettled up so as to preserve a good "top", the sight looking along the line of girders is extraordinary, for they rise and fall like waves of the sea! Sometimes things get so bad that the girders themselves have to be lifted.

The nature of steel enables such distortion to be taken up without any serious weakening of the structure, but it is far otherwise where masonry arches are concerned. At another big viaduct on the Taff Vale line the rate of subsidence is about one foot per year, and the piers supporting the arches seem to be tilting first and then sinking. The result is to produce a concertina effect, which causes the crowns of the arches to rise. To give extra support while subsidence is thus active the whole space beneath the arches is filled with a massive framework of heavy timbering. This reinforcing structure serves to show where movement is taking place. During such periods of subsidence structures likely to be affected are kept under the closest watch, and where necessary drastic speed restrictions are imposed.

Such are a few of the problems connected with the Road and its maintenance. As evidence of the increased burden to be carried, a heavy express train of fifty years ago weighed, with its locomotive, 350 to 400 tons, and its maximum speed was about 70 m.p.h.; in 1939 many of our important expresses were loading up to 700 tons, and attaining speeds up to 90 m.p.h. Today preparations are being made for regular running at 100 m.p.h. The smoothness of modern travel is the finest possible tribute to the manner in which the road is bearing its increased burden.

The lineside in the neighbourhood of large stations and goods yards does not usually provide a very edifying spectacle. Some twenty five years ago however, when the redoubtable John Miller was Engineer at York, the London and North Eastern Railway made a very welcome departure from the drab custom of the past, by initiating a definite scheme for beautifying the lineside. With the co-operation of a well-known firm of seedsmen, lawns were laid in the Vee space at junctions; liberal use was made of pre-cast concrete edging for the ballast and pathways, and new buildings, however humble their purpose, were designed by an architect. The fresh beauty of the lawns and the spick-and-span appearance of the fixed equipment transformed many a dreary site, while interest in the journey was stimulated by field and track signs indicating county boundaries, the halfway mark between London and Edinburgh, and such like. At the same time a very pleasing architectural style was developed in new buildings of major importance, such as the signal boxes at Thirsk, Leeds and Hull, and the Control Tower for the new marshalling yard at Hessle, also near Hull. The housing of fine modern equipment in buildings of such distinction naturally infused a renewed pride and enthusiasm which was reflected in the efficient working of the area as a whole.

In recent years the most careful attention has been paid to the architectural style of new railway buildings of importance, and some striking designs have been incorporated in modernized stations, signal boxes, restaurants, and even in booking offices. In addition to such officially planned adornment of the lineside the authorities at many country stations cultivate beautiful flower gardens, and these individual efforts are encouraged by the authorities through the holding of competitions for the most attractive displays. On the Great Western there were once at least two stretches where the lengthmen include some quite expert topiarists. Their work could be seen between Didcot and Pangbourne, on the Bristol main line, and also between Warminster and Salisbury, where bushes on the cutting sides have been attractively shaped—some into the form of birds.

At the present time a large proportion of British railway traffic is still operated by coal-fired steam locomotives, the basic principles of which have remained unaltered for more than a hundred years. This is not to stigmatize as unenterprising the work of past and present locomotive engineers, who have many times resorted to unorthodox design in the search for increased efficiency; it is rather an astounding tribute to the pioneer work of Trevithick and the Stephensons that their form of locomotive, gradually developed and enlarged, should still be one of the most reliable and generally useful forms of railway motive power yet devised.

In spite of the breathtaking speeds attained nowadays by other forms of transport and the introduction of many new diesels the steam locomotive continues to cast her spell upon young and old alike, though when comparison is made with alternative forms of railway traction many of her adherents reveal that some at least of their enthusiasm is based upon sentiment, and the undoubted fascination of a big steam locomotive seen in full action. It is therefore particularly interesting to hear the views of an eminent locomotive engineer who was one of the staunchest advocates of electrification. In his Presidential Address to the institution of Locomotive Engineers in 1944 the late Mr. W. S. Graff-Baker said:

"The steam locomotive as we know it is a machine with certain physical limitations and certain detrimental features. It is limited in power by the loading gauge, and in efficiency by the relatively limited temperature range. It has detrimental effects on the track and structures due to the extreme difficulty—or even impossibility—of obtaining a mechanical balance at varying speeds, and in this connexion it is only proper to observe that the track and structures are as essential parts of the railway as the locomotive. With these difficulties the fact remains that the steam locomotive is a magnificent machine, and has done more for the cause of civilization than any other effort of the mechanical engineer—far more than the internal combustion engine, which now seems to have a heavy debit as well as a credit entry in its balance sheet."

A handsome tribute indeed! Mr. Graff-Baker was Chief Mechanical Engineer to the London Passenger Transport Board, where it is of course unthinkable that anything but electric traction should be used. At the same time the conditions are very special: all passenger trains run at about the same speed; journeys are short, and the few goods trains are confined to the Metropolitan line, and run mostly at night. Except for a few residential trains on the Aylesbury line, which are hauled to Rickmansworth by electric locomotives, all London Transport passenger trains are made up on the multiple unit principle. Train units are made up in three- or four-car sets, and self-contained so far as motive power is concerned, as the electric motors are mounted on the coach bogies. When longer trains are required two or more sets are coupled together.

The intricate network of heavily-used lines converging upon the London terminal stations of the Southern Region provides a classic example of local electrification on the grand scale. Here again the multiple-unit system of train working has been used throughout. The Southern Region has demonstrated, however, that this method is not confined in its usefulness to purely suburban service. The main lines to Portsmouth, Brighton, Eastbourne, Ramsgate and Dover are now electrified, and the express trains, other than certain special continental boat services are all made up of multiple unit stock, corridor throughout, and including Pullman, buffet and full restaurant cars. These trains are of inestimable value at times of extreme pressure of traffic to the holiday resorts. At the London termini they require no shunting, or light engine movements; crews can be changed, restaurant cars re-victualled, and the trains re-loaded in a quarter of an hour, or twenty minutes at the most. At the busiest times the seating accomodation of the purely suburban train is increased by running two trailer cars behind a couple of four-car sets. The rapid acceleration of these local trains is often remarked upon, and it is not surprising in view of the power provided to operate them. The combined horsepower of the four units of a Southern ten-car suburban train totals up to 2,200, whereas a modern suburban steam locomotive rarely develops as much as 1,000 horsepower. The express train sets have a far greater power capacity—enough, indeed, to work a 12-car train up a gradient of 1 in 100 at nearly 60 m.p.h. In steam days unless the load was disproportionately light to the power of the locomotive one would be doing well to sustain 35 m.p.h., for example, on the long climb westwards out of the Medway valley to Sole Street.

Mr. Graff-Baker mentioned the ill-effects upon the

track and structures caused by steam locomotives, but I doubt whether these effects are so severe as those caused by multiple-unit electric trains. Certainly the coaches seem more prone to vibration on sections of the Southern Region where electric trains are run. In both the London Transport and Southern Region electrified systems direct current is used at a pressure of about 650 volts, and collected from conductor rails mounted on the permanent way. Some years ago a committee under the chairmanship of Lord Weir examined the whole field of railway electrification in Great Britain, and recommended that all future schemes should be equipped on the overhead wire system, using direct current at 1,500 volts. The Manchester to Sheffield line of the L.N.E.R. was electrified on this system; but now, the British Transport Commission has decided upon 25,000 volts, alternating current, as the standard for British Railways. The main line of the former London and North Western Railway between Manchester and Crewe has already been equipped; work on that between Liverpool and Crewe is well advanced, and work is now in hand for the extension southwards from Crewe to Euston. When the first edition of this book was published the idea of a change from the 1,500 volts. d.c. of the Weir committee was only being vaguely mooted, and I wrote: "as a result of certain technical developments, a strong plea is being made by experienced engineers for a reversal of that earlier decision. The circumstances of the Battle of the Gauges are recalled, and those of the more recent Battle of the Brakes; in this latter, expert opinion was irrevocably divided over the relative merits of the Westinghouse and Vacuum brakes. It may be that we shall witness a Battle of the Volts too!"

There is indeed a "battle of the volts", but it has taken a rather different form to that which might have been anticipated twenty years ago. There is little doubt that the system chosen by the British Transport Commission is the most efficient, technically, that modern engineering can provide; but its application to the cramped and crowded conditions of our busiest main lines has been fraught with a great number of incidental difficulties. To provide the necessary electrical clearances, many bridges have had to be raised; at Stockport a tunnel has had to be opened out, and these civil engineering works, combined with the large amount of work involved in the erection of the overhead supports for the high-tension wires have made the job of electrifying the lines from Crewe to Manchester and Liverpool a slow one. The process has been contrasted with the speed of extending the third-rail system of the Southern, first to Ramsgate and then to Dover, and the question has been asked many times whether it might not have been better to have a little less technical efficiency, and to get the job done and have the electric trains running in quicker time.

Here, indeed, are grounds for the continuation, in our modern age, of that spice of controversy in which connoisseurs of railway practice, both professional and amateur, have delighted in the past. Formerly it may have raged over compound *versus* simple steam locomotives, over rail gauges, over brakes, over carriage design or whether the chairs supporting bull-head rails should be screw-spiked, or bolted into the sleepers. Controversy apart, the new electric locomotives running on the London Midland Region are magnificent examples of modern engineering design, and I shall always remember vividly my first experience in the cab of one of them when we hauled a heavy train of 475 tons up to a maximum speed of 94 m.p.h. across the Cheshire Plain, and swept past another marvel of modern science, the great telescope at Jodrell Bank. These locomotives are designed to haul trains of this weight, representing thirteen or fourteen coaches of modern stock, between Manchester and London, and Liverpool and London at an average speed of 68 m.p.h. From what I have seen of their work already it would seem they will have a comfortable margin of power in reserve on such duties.

At the present time the whole picture of British railway motive power is changing: for apart from such notable schemes of electrification as the extension of the Southern system into East Kent, the main line projects from Manchester and Liverpool to Euston, the Great Eastern suburban lines, and the Glasgow scheme, on the north bank of the River Clyde, steam traction is being superseded by diesel on a wide scale. It is easy to wax sentimental, nostalgic, or indignant over this change; to point out the dangers of relying upon imported fuel, instead of using indigenous coal. But the sentimentalists, or those who would criticize on economic grounds have little knowledge of the state of affairs that had developed in the motive power departments on British Railways by the end of the second world war. During the lean years between 1930 and 1939 the railways had been starved of capital for the steady replacement, renovation, and modernization of equipment that is essential to keep any industry abreast of the times, and the very intensive use made of ageing equipment and locomotives during the war brought things almost to the pitch of complete break-down in certain areas.

The period of austerity and frustration following the end of the war hardly improved matters, and while the standards of express passenger running and locomotive maintenance vastly improved over the motive power stud as a whole, the attractions of employment in new and cleaner industries led to many hundreds of the younger men leaving the service. Although steam could still do the job, if it was in good condition and provided with reasonable fuel, and the crack express workings had lost none of their old glamour, there was no doubt it was outmoded for ordinary railway traction, and the decision to change over to diesel, as an urgent interim measure, prior to full electrification was a vital one. Apart from the diesel shunting locomotives, that are to be seen working in marshalling yards and goods stations throughout the length and breadth of the country, the main line locomotives fall into four broad power classifications. The "Type 4", which have an engine horsepower of 2000, and which are regularly working the principal expresses between Euston and Manchester, and Euston and Liverpool, can be classed as broadly equivalent in haulage capacity to the "Royal Scots", and the "Brittania" Pacifics. There is however this very important difference; the diesel gives of its best merely by having "the taps turned on", as it were, whereas the steam locomotive requires reasonably good coal, experienced firing, and good judgment from the driver. Of course I am only too well aware that a relatively small defect can put the diesel completely out of action, whereas a keen and experienced driver and fireman can coax a partially disabled steam locomotive through with very little loss of time. The engineering skill and "know-how" of British railway engineers are now being concentrated on the job of perfecting the performance of every detail of the diesels, so as to render to an absolute minimum the number of occasions on which failure occurs.

The fact that a diesel can be driven all-out for an indefinite time has enabled those responsible for allocation of engines to trains to put the Type 4 diesels on to express duties previously worked by steam locomotives of nominal greater power. On the Scottish expresses by the West Coast Route the big Stanier Pacifics of the "Duchess" class can considerably exceed the maximum output of the diesels, but conditions are not always favourable for their doing it. On the other hand the "Deltics" now being used on the East Coast Route are in a considerably higher power classification. They have some fifty per cent greater tractive power than the Type 4s, and are far more powerful than any of the existing steam locomotives on that route, or anywhere else in the country.

At the opposite end of the power scale are the handy little Type 2 diesels, having an engine horsepower of about 1,200, according to the various different detail designs now in service. These can be used singly on light trains, but in Scotland between Edinburgh and Aberdeen, and on the Highland main line between Perth and Inverness they are used in pairs. This is a useful and economic way of doubling up on the power available, for unlike a steam train that is double-headed there is no need to provide a second engine crew. The two locomotives are coupled in multiple unit, and operated by one crew. The Type 2 locomotives are extensively used in East Anglia for the intermediate jobs, and where the principal express duties are performed by locomotives of Type 3 capacity. In this part of the country Type 4 locomotives, of the same design as those working heavy expresses from Euston, are mainly employed on express freight work, thus exemplifying their versatility.

Even in these days of increasing standardization however, uniformity is not yet spreading over the whole country. It is true that the same type of diesel-electric locomotive—a Type 4 of the "D.200" class—can be seen hauling the Flying Scotsman, an express from Euston to Liverpool, an East Anglian freight, or taking a London to Glasgow express up the Beattock bank. But one feels the shade of Brunel would have smiled when his successors on the Great Western decided, for their motive power modernization, to do something different from all the rest of the country. The spirit of the broad gauge days on the Great Western never seems to have quite died away: the spirit of individualism, the desire to have something for their very own may not have been uppermost in the minds of those responsible, but in point of fact while every other part of Great Britain accepted electric transmission for the new diesel locomotives the Western Region decided upon hydraulic.

The "Warship" class of diesel-hydraulic express locomotives may not have the glamour of the old Great Western "Kings" and "Castles", but they are doing some very good work, and at this stage one would be rash to try to form any opinion as to whether the hydraulic drive of the Western Region, or the electric drive used elsewhere, is the better proposition. Both designs are extremely economical on fuel. Motorists who are conscious of the "miles per gallon" of their cars may well open their eyes to hear that in hauling 14 and 15 coach express trains between London and Liverpool the Type 4 diesel-electrics use about one gallon of fuel oil per mile. The Western locomotives are all named after ships of the Royal Navy, and it so happens that not a few of those chosen have previously been borne by famous Great Western locomotives of the steam age. There is no doubt about it that their names—and the numbers of the diesel-electrics on other regions—are being collected as eagerly by the younger generation, as their fathers looked out for *King Henry V*, *Queen Berengaria*, or *Nunney Castle*, or as their grandfathers extolled the glories of the broad gauge. As the pageant of locomotive development rolls on, indeed, the number of enthusiasts seems to grow rather than diminish.

Steam is now very rapidly on the way out. In addition to the displacement of famous express locomotives by diesels on the crack trains a great number of local services have been changed over to multiple-unit railcar sets, while the multiple-unit principle, so successfully exploited on the Southern Region electrified system, has been applied with equally good results to certain medium distance express services, such as Edinburgh to Glasgow, Birmingham to South Wales, and Liverpool to Hull. There still remains a preponderance of steam on the heaviest freight services, while in many areas steam goods locomotives of widely varying vintages are engaged on numerous humdrum, bread and butter jobs that will remain for many years occult from the glamour of diesel operation. Goods engines in general deserve honourable mention, because they so seldom "hit the headlines" in stories of railway operation.

I was on Shrewsbury station one day in the autumn of 1944 when I heard the heavy beat of a wheezy old engine. Soon there appeared, running tender first, a veteran London and North Western 0–6–0, of the class known officially as the "17 inch coal engines". This old harridan was built 61 years earlier, and here she came spluttering through on a train of some forty wagons, a transfer goods between marshalling yards at the north and south end of the station. In strong contrast are the powerful modern examples of the 0–6–0 type, such as Sir Nigel Gresley's "J.39" class on the L.N.E.R. and the "4000" class of the former Midland Railway, which was adopted as an L.M.S. standard. But the variety which has attracted by far the most attention by reason of its unorthodox appearance, is the Southern "austerity" engine, built in 1942 to the designs of Mr. O. V. S. Bulleid. In producing this weird, though very efficient machine, under the most severe wartime conditions, the object was to use the very minimum of metal, and at the same time to put upon the road an engine on which maintenance work could be carried out with the least possible trouble. In doing so convention was thrown to the winds.

There is no doubt that the great majority of persons who "worship at the shrine of the steam locomotive"—to use a notable phrase of the late Mr. Loughnan Pendred—were horrified at the appearance of Mr. Bulleid's goods engine, known officially as Class "Q1". There is, after all, artistry in engineering, and quite apart from superficial adornments many locomotives have what Mr. Henry Maxwell has termed "a balanced plastic symmetry" that is pleasing to the eye. But in locomotive engineering as in other arts there is more than one school of thought, and so far as outward appearance goes the "Q1" engines can be considered as an expression, in a locomotive, of the cubist, or surrealist school.

The heaviest goods and mineral trains in this country are mostly worked by engines having eight wheels coupled; but although this class is generally larger and more powerful than the 0–6–0 type, British freight locomotives taken as a whole are small in relation to the loading of the trains. This characteristic is due, strangely enough, to the lack of brake power on the wagons. It would not be safe to work up to 45 or 50 m.p.h. with a coal train weighing 1,000 tons. Furthermore the wagons are loose-coupled, and in starting the engine picks up the load, so to speak, a little at a time; with a really long train of 70 or 80 wagons the locomotive is well under way by the time the last vehicles are started from rest. Speeds while on the run do not much exceed 30 m.p.h., and a trip of 74 miles from Peterborough to the London distribution yards at Hornsey may, even under the most favourable conditions, take seven hours or more. The process of fitting all wagons with continuous brakes is a slow one, and the long slow-moving goods train is likely to be with us for many years.

In mentioning that these 0–8–0s are essentially slow-speed machines I am reminded of an amusing occurrence during the investigations of the Bridge Stress Committee in 1923–5. Bridges in various parts of the country were being tested firstly to observe, by scientific measurement, the vibrational characteristics of the bridges themselves due to the passage of locomotives or trains, and secondly to observe how the oscillation varied when different types of locomotive were run across. Tests were in progress on a certain bridge in the North of England, and an express engine of the local company made a series of runs—faster each time—till finally she flashed across at 92 m.p.h. Then came the turn of a heavy three-cylinder 0–8–0 mineral engine. She made several runs at normal speed, in each case running without any train behind her, and then some of the eminent scientists present asked the driver to make a really fast run. The worthy man took a great deal of persuading, but eventually he agreed to "have a go"; it was a "go" indeed for he brought that great lumbering cart-horse of an engine tearing over the bridge at 59 m.p.h.! The Committee were delighted; so was the driver. But what the locomotive authorities said about it when the tale came to their ears is best not recorded here.

Modern eight-coupled freight locomotives can develop speeds of 60 m.p.h. with ease, but it is perhaps fitting that the class that has the nostalgic honour of including the very last steam locomotive to be built for service on the railways of Britain has proved speedworthy to an extent that would have seemed incredible to us even when the first edition of this book was published. In the series of standard steam locomotives built for British Railways since nationalization is a heavy freight, with the 2–10–0 wheel arrangement. It has a large boiler of roughly the same size as that of the "Britannia" Pacific, but the coupled wheels are only 5 ft. in diameter, as compared with the usual 6 ft. 6 in., or even larger, of express passenger locomotives. These fine engines, Class 9F as they are known, do a multitude of heavy freight jobs. They haul the ore trains from Newport docks up to Ebbw Vale, coal trains on the Midland line, and on Saturdays in the summer they take turns on the relief passenger and excursion trains. On test runs from Swindon one of them reached speeds of more than 75 m.p.h. The climax was reached however one afternoon on the Great Northern main line south of Grantham. The train was the "Flying Scotsman" southbound from Edinburgh, and at the time of this particular journey a stop was made at Grantham to change engines. An expert recorder of train speeds was travelling by the express, but he did not leave his seat to see the fresh engine. There would be time enough to get its number on arrival at King's Cross. The run that followed was an exceedingly good one, with some very fast running on the favourable stretches of line and a maximum speed of 90 m.p.h. near Essendine. Imagine that recorder's astonishment when King's Cross was reached, and he discovered that the engine from Grantham had not been a "Pacific" at all, but a "9F"

2–10–0 goods engine! The last of this class to be built, the very last steam locomotive, is named *Evening Star*.

Nowadays, one must, perforce, write of the great achievements of British express passenger steam locomotives almost entirely in the past tense, and while studying the work of the new electrics and diesels with the diligence that their importance demands, the feats of their predecessors become even more vivid memories. For my own part the bare facts of hundreds of journeys —some on the footplate, and many more as a passenger —are contained in dozens of cherished notebooks, some bearing ample evidence of the footplate in their greasy, spattered pages. But mere figures can give no impression of a steam locomotive in full action. I have ridden the Great Western "Kings" and "Castles" at speeds up to nearly 100 m.p.h.; I have seen the Southern "Merchant Navy" Pacifics develop nearly two thousand horsepower at the drawbar; I have ridden every mile of the L.M.S from Euston to Aberdeen, and to Inverness and Wick, and have been on a Gresley "A4" Pacific at 103 m.p.h. But even the great thrill of speed, seen and sensed from the engine itself, forms only a small part of the compelling atmosphere of the footplate.

One afternoon before the war I was travelling south by the "Flying Scotsman". It was winter time and the light was beginning to fade unusually early, and the snow which we had run through at intervals on the way south from Edinburgh began to come on in earnest after Grantham. I had been glad enough to travel passenger for most of the way, but for the last stage of the journey I donned overalls, a sweat-rag and an old cap, and went

99

up towards the front end. In the train it was tea time, and under the soft shaded lights of a dining car decorated in the style of a French drawing room of the Louis XVI period the white coated stewards were hurrying to and fro. But then, after groping my way through the narrow, pitch-dark passage that led from the gangway connexion of the leading coach through one side of the tender I came to the footplate. The speed was already in the fifties. On some engines that I have known the racket would have been ear-splitting; others would be rolling and lurching, but this was *Quicksilver*, one of Sir Nigel Gresley's "A4" Pacifics, riding like a real lady.

There was, I must immediately add, no drawing-room atmosphere about the cab of that powerful engine. In the brilliant arc of light from the firedoor the fireman stoked deftly and fast; up in the shades on the left the driver sat looking out ahead into the dusk; coal dust was flying—an occasional spray of the water hose to keep it down—and in a very few seconds I had settled down to that most strangely compelling and fascinating mode of travel, roasted down one side, ice-cold the other, and rapidly getting a very dirty face! There was no time to pay any attentions to such minor incidentals, for *Quicksilver* was running the "Flying Scotsman", with fifteen heavy coaches behind her, and with no more than 107 minutes in which to cover the 105½ miles from Grantham to King's Cross. Stoke Tunnel had been passed and we were on the gentle down grade towards Peterborough: regulator full open, but valve gear linked up so as to use the steam expansively. There was not a sound from the exhaust; no lurching and swaying, just the "sing" of the wheels over the rail joints and the occasional clang of the shovel. Seventy, then, eighty, and then ninety miles per hour! The snow seemed to be driving well-nigh level as we tore down through Essendine and over the fen country past Tallington; but fortunately the signal lights stood out clear through the storm, and we were able to run at normal speed. Yes, that was the normal speed of the "Flying Scotsman" on that stretch in the greatest days of steam.

As a lineside spectacle, particularly in high summer when there is less tendency for the exhaust steam to condense, these streamlined trains were impressive only in the apparent absence of effort with which they swept along. Generally speaking the modern steam locomotive is most spectacular when working hard up a heavy gradient. There is a fascination in the gradual approach to mountain country, in the swing of the track from side to side, up a winding valley, in the slackening speed, and the noisier exhaust beat, till finally there comes the triumphant pull over the summit in some deep mountain pass. There are many Scottish lines on which that peculiar thrill can be experienced, but one meets it too on the Welsh border. I had ridden up from Devonshire on the engine of a Great Western express from Plymouth to Liverpool, and soon after Leominster hills came crowding into the picture seen through the cab glasses. Ludlow, the Clee Hills, Stokesay Castle, passed in fascinating procession; and then, with the heights of Caer Caradoc and the Long Mynd ahead of us, the driver opened out his gleaming "Castle" engine to make a superb climb to the summit in the pass near Church Stretton. In such surroundings the steady rhythmical beat, an occasional sight of our 14-coach train winding round the curves behind us, and the spectacle of an engine completely master of its job, made a splendid climax to the whole journey, and one which the subsequent 75 m.p.h. dash down to Shrewsbury did nothing to destroy.

Even in the days of streamlined Pacifics the Great Western 4–6–0s of the "Castle" class ranked among the most outstanding engines on British metals. Churchward by his invaluable pioneer work may well be called the father of the modern British locomotive and it was by the "Castle" class—a development of his epoch-making design of 1907—that convincing evidence of Great Western prowess was carried to the northern lines. Certainly the experimental running of *Pendennis Castle* on the L.N.E.R. in 1925 and of *Launceston Castle* on the L.M.S Railway in 1926 proved a turning point in the locomotive history of both these companies. Not for the first time in its history, however, the Great Western awoke others to excel it, this time in the haulage power and speed of its express locomotives.

On the L.N.E.R., Gresley having altered the valve gear of his Pacific engines to make them certainly the equal of, if not superior to the "Castles", developed the design to an extraordinary degree in the next eleven years. Two runs over that magnificent, straight and virtually level road from Northallerton to York will illustrate this point. On the first, *Flying Scotsman*, an engine of the earliest Pacific design, but fitted with the improved valve gear, made a flying average speed of 72.4 m.p.h. over a certain 26-mile stretch; this was achieved with a

16-coach train weighing 565 tons behind the tender. On the second run, one of the latest streamlined engines, then named *Capercaillie,* but since renamed *Sir Charles Newton,* pulled off a remarkable average of 75.9 m.p.h. over the same stretch of line with a colossal wartime load of 21 coaches weighing no less than 730 tons behind the tender. This latter run indicates a haulage power some 35 per cent. greater, although *Capercaillie* is only 10 per cent. heavier than *Flying Scotsman.*

The latest of the L.N.E.R. streamlined engines, of which the *Sir Charles Newton* is an example, include an important variation in the layout of the blastpipe and chimney. Hitherto locomotive designers had always been in somewhat of a cleft stick so far as blastpipe proportions were concerned. If one increased the size of the nozzle to get a free exhaust and a fast running engine the blast was not fierce enough to draw the fire, and the boiler would not steam. If one reduced the size of the nozzle to sharpen up the blast, the exhaust would be choked, and the engine would not run fast. So the actual design was always something of a compromise. By adaptation of the double chimney used on certain French engines, Gresley secured unprecedented freedom of exhaust, combined with good steaming. Similarly on the Southern Railway, Mr. Bulleid had improved the work of the "Lord Nelson" class 4–6–0s and the "Schools" class 4–4–0s, by fitting them with multiple-jet blastpipes, having five nozzles instead of the usual one; and the same arrangement was used in his "air-smoothed" Pacific engines of the "Merchant Navy" class.

On the L.M.S Railway progress was no less striking.

Here the influence of Swindon is even more apparent, though not surprising, seeing that Sir William Stanier, who was Chief Mechanical Engineer from 1932 to 1944, had, prior to his appointment, spent the whole of his professional career in the service of the Great Western Railway. His Pacific engines, whether streamlined or otherwise, worked through from London to Glasgow— a continuous run of 401 miles—and have set up many fine records. These include a non-stop run from Glasgow to Euston at an average speed of 70 m.p.h., with a special test train of 8 coaches, and an even more startling run from Crewe to Euston, again with a load of 8 coaches, on which the average speed from start to stop was 79.9 m.p.h. On one test journey a speed of 114 m.p.h. was attained. At the invitation of the L.M.S Railway I was a passenger on this particular test, and the high speed was run between Whitmore and Crewe. We passed over the summit near Whitmore at exactly 85 m.p.h. There was just a purr from the engine, it might have been the exhaust, and might not; be that as it may the next few minutes were very thrilling. It was all over so quickly that one formed no lasting impression. I was dimly conscious of the coach swaying gently from side to side; of the wheel beats coming faster and faster; of my companion sitting opposite waiting almost breathlessly for me to call out the result of each stop-watch reading; all the time my face was glued to the window sighting and clocking the whizzing mileposts. Madeley station, 2.6 miles beyond Whitmore was passed at 97 m.p.h.; another mile and we were over the hundred; and from that faster and faster until I clocked two successive half miles in precisely 16 seconds each—112½ m.p.h. Then we were tearing past Crewe sorting sidings, braking hard, and a moment later were at rest in the station. The chart on the speed recorder of the locomotive showed a peak rate of 114 m.p.h. The latest engines of this class were fitted with double chimneys, and some of these locomotives and their crews did not even wait for the end of the war to show what they can do. The *King George VI*, working a 15-coach northbound train, was stopped by signal on the Grayrigg bank; on getting the road once more, and starting this big load in the middle of a mountain gradient, the engine accelerated to *sixty miles per hour* in six miles from rest, and cleared the summit of the Grayrigg incline, on a gradient of 1 in 106 at 55 m.p.h.

CARRIAGES AND WAGONS

The "wheel" of railway carriage design in Great Britain shows a striking tendency to come full circle. In the earliest days third class passengers were conveyed in open trucks, herded as closely together as they could be packed in seatless pens. Improvements came very slowly —grudgingly, indeed it would seem, from the manner in which the railway companies at first sought to evade requirements laid down in the Regulation of Railways Acts in 1844. For many years the idea of the communal third class carriage lingered, and even after the seats had been arranged transversely after the fashion of the first and second class compartments, the partitions were carried only just high enough to provide a rest for the back. Less than twenty years ago there were third class carriages running in the London suburban area, with plain boards for seats, and the partitions stopping just above the head-level of a seated passenger.

Generally however third class passengers had enjoyed the comparative privacy of separate compartments at a much earlier date, and the kind of accommodation originally exclusive to the first class could be considered as standard on the British railways some twenty years ago. Since the grouping, however, the communal carriage has enjoyed a remarkable revival, albeit in the pleasant modern form of the open saloons with centre vestibule. Especially attractive among these were the excursion train coaches of the L.N.E.R., externally distinctive in a livery of apple green and cream, and comfortably furnished with bucket seats, deep windows and tables for four. These coaches are representative of yet another marked trend in British railway carriage design—the abandonment of separate doors for each compartment in the main line corridor stock.

On services where stops are frequent separate doors are generally being retained, so as to permit of quick loading and unloading of passengers; but on many recent carriages intended for long distance express trains there are doors only at the ends. This departure from established British practice has made possible the single deep windows in the compartments which are so splendid for seeing the countryside. Although constructional practice has advanced considerably in the use of all-welded steel frames, the interior decoration of carriages has remained traditional in its use of wood panelling, and wooden doors. This gives a feeling of solidarity and homeliness that is absent from all-steel coaches; on the Continent the clang of steel doors both to platform and the corridor strikes a jarring note. The L.M.S Railway gave an added interest to their latest main line coaches by fixing labels giving the names of the Home or Empire timber from which the panelling of the particular coach is made.

Perhaps the most beautiful scheme of interior decoration ever applied to a British railway carriage was that used in the restaurant cars of the "Flying Scotsman" until 1938. They were decorated after the style of a Louis XVI drawing-room, in delicate shades of pink intermingled with white and grey. The beauty of those cars was never seen to better effect than at tea on a winter afternoon, when the soft shaded table lights were on, and the white-coated stewards were bustling to and fro. One such occasion remains a particularly vivid memory, when, as mentioned earlier in this chapter I went straight from the cosy pleasance through the corridor tender, to the harsh and contrasting glamour of the footplate!

The business men of Manchester are justly famed for their good fellowship, and the stranger would no doubt be astonished to discover how much business in the cotton industry is conducted in the congenial atmosphere of the City's many coffee houses. For the benefit of season-ticket holders travelling in daily from Blackpool, the former Lancashire and Yorkshire Railway introduced club cars on certain important business expresses. These cars were reserved for members, who paid an annual subscription for the privilege. In 1939 club cars were run on four morning expresses from Blackpool to Manchester, some for first-class and others for third-class passengers; these cars returned on business expresses leaving Manchester between 5 and 6 o'clock in the evening. There were also club carriages run on services operated by the former London and North Western Railway between Manchester and Llandudno.

Another interesting departure from the conventional form of passenger carriage was made on the South Eastern Railway in 1892, when six parlour cars were purchased from the Gilbert Car Company, of Troy, U.S.A., and run as individual units in some of the principal expresses. Later these cars were brought together to form an "all-parlour" train on the London-Hastings service, and although first-class only when introduced in 1892 the arrangements were modified to provide first, second and third class accommodation when all six cars were grouped together as one train. With their great curtained windows, high, decorated clerestory roofs and the appurtenances of a typical Victorian drawing-room these cars certainly struck a highly distinctive note among the sombre compartment stock of that period.

Although since 1876 Pullman cars had been run on various day trains in the south of England it was the inception, in November 1908, of the first daily all-Pullman train that set the final seal upon the popularity of these cars. The train was the *Southern Belle* of the London Brighton and South Coast Railway, running non-stop from Victoria to Brighton in exactly one hour. Four times a day the Sussex countryside was adorned by the passage of this stately train, the umber and cream coaches harmonizing perfectly with the Vandyke-brown of the engine. Originally the train carried first class passengers only, but the third class Pullmans introduced elsewhere on the Brighton system proved so popular that they were included in the *Southern Belle* in 1921. At the same time the Brighton, like its near neighbour the South Eastern and Chatham, operated no corridor stock at all in its main line trains, and even on the relatively short runs from London to Brighton, Eastbourne or Portsmouth cars in which a variety of refreshments could be obtained were sure of a welcome.

In railway travel luxury alone has not attracted much business in Great Britain. In 1929 an all-Pullman train was introduced between London, Torquay and Paignton; it left Paddington at 11 a.m., just one hour before the ordinary Great Western express "The Torbay Limited". The Pullman train, for which supplementary fares had to be paid, took ten minutes longer on the run down than the well-established and very popular flyer; it may be argued that a difference of ten minutes is very small in a run of $3\frac{1}{2}$ hours, but the only incentive to travel by the new service was the luxury of the accommodation. It was a complete failure. On the other hand the London and North Eastern Pullman trains proved a great success, because they provided the additional attraction of increased speed. This was particularly so between Leeds and King's Cross. The southbound "Queen of Scots", for example, on its journey from Glasgow to London, left Leeds at about 4 p.m.—a most convenient departure time for business men—and was always heavily patronised.

A Pullman car of unusual design was built in 1914 for service on the Caledonian Railway. This was equipped with a buffet for the serving of light meals, but the rear end was constructed as an observation lounge with deep armchairs, and huge windows extending from floor to ceiling. This car, named "Maid of Morven" was run as the last vehicle of the 9.45 a.m. express from Glasgow to Oban, returning by the corresponding afternoon train. It was a wonderful experience to travel through the sublime mountain scenery of the West Highlands in this car. Both the London and North Western, and the Cambrian Railways ran observation cars on certain routes in North Wales, but most striking of all these special vehicles were the beaver-tail observation cars designed by Sir Nigel Gresley for the Coronation streamlined expresses of the L.N.E.R. They formed not only a very striking tail to the train but also assisted in reducing air resistance at high speed. While the outlook from these beautiful cars is much the same as that experienced in the "Maid of Morven", one had on the Coronation the thrill of high-speed main line travel. I have the most vivid recollections of one particular journey: how curious it was to see signals being put to danger behind us, and to watch expresses go racing by on the other road! Owing to a sea mist there was little to be glimpsed in the way of scenery, but the very dampness of the air produced a most interesting exposition of the effect of the tail-end streamlining. Exhaust steam from the engine was all the time coming in clouds; a certain proportion was deflected sideways, but when the wind and our direction were favourable smoke passed throughout the length of the train, along the carriage roofs, and on reaching the tail was drawn down in a smooth stream without a suspicion of swirls and eddies. One has only to watch a train with an ordinary upright back running through fog to see the disturbance created in its wake; the contrast in the case of the "Coronation" was strikingly revealed in this moist air.

Since the nationalization of British Railways the design of coaching stock has remained more or less traditional, but quite recently some new high speed Pullman trains have been put on, running from Birmingham, from Bristol, and from Manchester to London. These trains are built on the multiple-unit principle, like the Southern electrics, and are diesel-powered. Externally the trains are strikingly styled in a colour scheme of blue and white, while internally the open-saloon type of car, with a table in front of every seat has been retained in an ultra-modern form of seating and decor. They are air-conditioned, and travel in them is very quiet and free from the excessive heat or cold that it is sometimes difficult to avoid with ordinary saloon type carriages. The speeds maintained overall are good, though anyone expecting a special thrill in the way of maximum speed would be disappointed. Such is the margin of power built into these trains that time is gained on the uphill sections and there is no need to indulge in anything very spectacular on the favourable stretches of line.

The observation cars run in pre-war days on the Coronation express included a lock-up compartment for the conveyance of mails, but the design of vans and coaches purely for mail traffic forms a most interesting

111

study in itself. The travelling post office was introduced as long ago as 1838, and in the same year the earliest experiments were made on a converted horsebox with apparatus for picking up and dropping mail bags while running. In the following year the first post office sorting carriage to be equipped with this apparatus was built by the Grand Junction Railway. It was however some years before this clever device had been made sufficiently reliable to be worked at full speed, and it was not until the year 1854 that it came into regular use on the Irish Mail. Nowadays the special mail trains running between Euston and Aberdeen usually include no less than six of these sorting tenders.

The special postal expresses were introduced in 1885 jointly by the London and North Western and the Caledonian Railways, and even today the names of these original companies are perpetuated in the postmarks on letters stamped in the travelling post offices: "North Western T.P.O. Night Down", "Caledonian T.P.O. Day Down", and so on. In normal times no fewer than 35 sorters travel by the 8.30 p.m. express from Euston, and at important centres such as Bletchley and Nuneaton five, six or seven pouches are collected at 65–70 m.p.h. from the lineside standards. The sorting vans each have four traductors for the delivery of pouches, and sometimes as many as eighteen pouches are set down at one lineside net. Up to the outbreak of war some mail for Ireland was regularly sorted on the Scottish mail train. After sorting, this matter was made up into bags and delivered to the ground nets at certain specified places; there, the postman transferred them from the nets to the lineside

112

standards, and they were then collected, also at full speed, by the Irish Mail some twenty minutes later. The Irish Mail itself, a heavy and popular sleeping car express, carried only two sorting carriages, and this interesting procedure greatly relieved the work of the sorters. The only other exclusively postal train in Great Britain is the West of England mail operated by the Western Region between Paddington and Penzance.

In 1904 the Great Western built some very large stowage vans for overseas postal traffic arriving at Plymouth. This purpose was made plain for all the world to see by the legend OCEAN MAILS painted in huge letters on the coach bodies. Some of these fine vehicles began their career most auspiciously, by running in the train that made the record run from Plymouth to London in May 1904, travelling at over 100 m.p.h. on one section of the line. The Great Western used distinctive names for all classes of covered wagons, and many of these seem inappropriate till one realizes that they are merely code words by which members of the staff recognize instantly the class of wagon required. The principle has been extended since nationalization to other sections of British Railways. Of these names "*Siphon*," "*Macaw*", "*Bloater*" and "*Dogfish*" are typical examples.

The Great Western broke new ground in 1936 by using a diesel-engined railcar for express parcel traffic between London and Oxford. Its first run every morning, an express trip, was from Kensington, Addison Road station, carrying confectionery from the Cadby Hall depot of J. Lyons & Co., to Reading and Oxford. Before nationalization the Great Western was the only railway in Britain to make extensive use of diesel railcars for passenger traffic; these partly streamlined vehicles, with the fine look-out, pleasing decoration, smooth riding, and speeds up to 70 m.p.h. have proved very popular. The oil-engined rail-car, sometimes operating a really fast service, is a modern development of the steam "rail motor cars" that were so much in vogue thirty years ago. These latter were mostly intended for branch line service, and consisted of a tiny steam locomotive and a single coach built on to one chassis. They were slow running and not very adaptable to varying traffic requirements; but for a time they served a useful purpose in a period when the railways had little or no competition in rural districts. Since nationalization the diesel railcar, running in multiple unit, has become the standard type of train for branch line and local services.

Comment is often made upon the comparative smallness of the wagons used in ordinary goods service, but a number of factors combine to make the humble four-wheeler by far the most convenient for general service under the conditions existing in this country. First of all much of the freight carried by the British railways consists of small consignments. Then, in earlier railway days a very great number of sidings were laid out in factories, collieries, and such public utility establishments as gas works and electric power stations, where lack of space led to the use of sharp curves and narrow clearances, only just adequate for small four-wheeled wagons. The small wagon is easy to handle; at country stations where locomotives are not often available for shunting they can be pushed by hand, if need be.

For special through goods traffic a variety of high capacity wagons have been built, notably the 40-ton all-steel bogie coal wagons on the L.M. Region for taking fuel to the Stonebridge Park power station, and the bogie wagons used for the heavy brick traffic on the L.N.E.R. from Peterborough to London. An interesting example of smaller wagons specially designed for a particular traffic is provided by the glass-lined tank wagons used by the United Dairies, Ltd., for the conveyance of milk. For loads of exceptional size and bulk what are termed well-wagons are used; they consist of no more than a platform on to which the load is fixed down. As many of these special loads are bulky the central portion of the truck between the bogie is sunk so as to give greater headroom.

Sometimes the railways are called upon to carry an article of such bulk as to extend beyond the ordinary limits of loading. Then special arrangements have to be made to ensure that the adjoining railway tracks are not in use at the time the exceptional load is due to pass. Usually such a consignment is operated as a special train; while it is running on the left hand track it will overhang the right hand one and the greatest care has to be taken in selecting a route where the least possible dislocation of traffic will be caused by the temporary closing of one line. The L.M.S Railway once conveyed a complete automatic telephone exchange; in another instance signal arms and workmen's huts had to be removed temporarily to allow an exceptionally bulky load to pass. One of the strangest jobs of this kind came in 1942 when a large works near London contributed an 85-ton block of solid steel to the wartime scrap metal collection. This had previously done duty as the block of a giant steam hammer, and upon the Great Western fell the task of loading it and arranging for its conveyance to a north-country steel-breakers' yard.

And so finally we come to the tail end. One does not look for luxury in the guard's brake van of a goods train, but it can all the same be a fascinating place. On a warm summer night I rode in the van of an express goods from Manchester to Carlisle, and from the open platform at the rear, in brilliant moonlight, saw the fine mountain scenery of the northern Pennines in a strange new guise. Exhilarating too was our 60 m.p.h. run down to Carlisle. But on this train all the wagons were fitted with the continuous brake, and the couplings were screwed tight; our running, though boisterous at times, was free from the violent jerks and clangings usually associated with the operation of goods trains. One has to travel in the van of a loose-coupled unbraked train to appreciate the buffetings that occur sometimes, and the driver who makes a quick get-away will certainly not be popular with his guard!

CONTROL OF TRAFFIC

It seems a far cry nowadays to the time of the policemen stationed at intervals along the line to regulate the slow-moving traffic of the early railways. From those primitive beginnings the art of signalling has developed, slowly at times, very rapidly at others, until today it is one of the most fascinating branches of railway engineering. Its functions have been notably extended in recent years. At first signals were installed purely in the interests of safety, to inform the driver when the line ahead was obstructed, and by a different indication to tell him when it was safe to proceed. Today, while safety in working is still the primary consideration, signalling has come to be regarded as one of the most important aids towards speeding up and intensifying the train services.

But with all the modern refinements of remote electric controls, audible signals in the locomotive cab, and so on, the whole edifice of British signalling still rests upon the sure foundation of the Block System, first introduced in 1841, through Clay Cross Tunnel on the North Midland Railway. This great principle—dividing the line up into sections, and allowing only one train at a time in any one section—is inherently safe, and yet it is surprising how strongly it was opposed in certain quarters, and for how long afterwards the method of allowing trains to follow one after another after a certain interval of time remained in use. The first railway to be equipped from end to end on the space interval system was the oft-derided South Eastern; they were using it as early as 1851. In our tolerant British style individual railway companies were allowed to go their diverse ways, though gradually the principle of the "space interval" gained general acceptance. Nevertheless progress in equipping the various lines was leisurely, until, in 1889, there occurred a terrible accident near Armagh; at this public opinion was so shocked that an Act of Parliament was passed compelling all the railways to work on the Block System.

In remote districts where trains are few and a double line of railway is not justified the Block System is elaborated to guard against the dire possibilities of a head-on collision. A driver is not only given a signal to proceed; he is also issued with a "token" as his authority to use the line. The token sometimes takes the form of a staff, and on other lines a circular steel tablet is used. But even in these regions of sparse traffic there are some express trains; the Highland mails run up to 70 m.p.h., in places, between Perth and Inverness, and time cannot be spared to stop at the passing loops to give up the token for one section, and receive that for the next. The job of exchanging tokens while running through a passing loop usually devolved upon the fireman, and while it was nothing to throw out the old one the intrepid Scottish lads grew expert in hooking on to their arm the hoop of the leather pouch containing the new token.

This "smash and grab" act is usually performed at about 15 m.p.h., except when the driver happens to be in a hurry. The experienced fireman could take it well enough; some, indeed, on occasions of late running, urged their mates to go through faster still, though one fine day on the Stranraer line a young fellow so misjudged things as to try and embrace the bag of the water column. He went head over heels clean out of the cab, mercifully without serious injury. Conditions were vastly improved after 1890 by James Manson's invention of apparatus for the automatic exchange of tokens. Manson was Locomotive Engineer of the Great North of Scotland Railway, and this apparatus was also adopted by the neighbouring Highland Line, where today the ex-

118

change is regularly made at 60 m.p.h. In many hundreds of miles of travelling over lines fitted with this apparatus I have known only one exchange foozled. I was travelling on the engine at the time, and a lively thirty seconds we had! Approaching the loop the driver attempted to swing out the catcher, when to his consternation it was jammed; mighty blows with the hammer failed to release it, and by that time, travelling at 50 m.p.h., we had run past the exchange standard. There was nothing for it but to stop and send the hapless fireman back to collect the token.

Still more awkward circumstances might have arisen from an accident that occurred "somewhere in Wessex" a few years ago. On a line where exchanging is done by hand the fireman made a bad shot, and merely knocked the pouch upwards off the standard. It ricochetted off the side of the engine cab, rolled down the high embankment and disappeared into some long grass. The train was stopped and the fireman went in search; not finding it immediately he was followed by the driver, and then the guard. For ten minutes or so this trio was busily engaged fishing in the grass, for a lost token is a serious matter. One cannot follow cricket procedure, chalk up a "six", and get a fresh one, for the block instruments at each end of the section are electrically interlocked and it is impossible to extract another token while one is still out. Fortunately the lost one was found, otherwise pilot working would have had to have been introduced.

Pilot working is most frequently seen during temporary single-line operation, as on Sundays when relaying of the permanent way is in progress. On a double line of railway while one road is under renewal the other road must carry all the traffic in both directions. A pilotman is appointed, and he must personally authorise every train movement over the section. He rides on the engine of each train, except when two or more trains are going through in the same direction; in this latter case he travels on the last of the group. I saw an interesting case of pilot working during a Sunday journey from Shrewsbury to Bristol. South of Hereford the train took the alternative, though less used route via Ross and Gloucester, and our driver had with him an experienced local engineman as a road pilot. Between Grange Court and Gloucester relaying was in progress, and for a short distance we had on the footplate a second pilotman, for the temporary single-line section.

At an early date in railway history it was felt that some positive safeguard was required against the chance of signalmen pulling the wrong levers. In the autumn of 1895 the Hampstead branch of the North London Railway was completed, and Colonel Yolland made the inspection on behalf of the Board of Trade. He was not satisfied with the arrangements at Kentish Town Junction, and requested that some mechanism be installed to prevent the lowering of the wrong signal. The engineer, Austin Chambers, assured him that it would be done, and in November of that year the Colonel came again. He was shown that if the signalman put his foot in the stirrup to lower the main line signal the corresponding stirrup for the branch signal was disengaged, so that the latter could not be lowered. The Inspector agreed, and was shown also that the converse interlocking held good too. The railway officials thereupon waited for the expected Government blessing; instead, Colonel Yolland stepped forward, pressed down both stirrups at once and lowered the main and branch line signals simultaneously! So Austin Chambers had to try again, for the Colonel naturally refused to sanction the opening of the line.

In his method of testing the primitive interlocking at Kentish Town Junction Colonel Yolland established an invaluable precedent. In seeking possible chances of error he went completely outside the ordinary operational routine, and found a serious weakness. His action had the effect, everywhere in the country, of putting signal engineers "on their toes", so to speak, and since then the greatest care has always been lavished on interlocking mechanisms. For more than sixty years afterwards the interlocking between signal and point levers was done by purely mechanical means. Nowadays however such rapid developments are taking place in the art of electric interlocking that it is difficult to imagine what form the control machine will have taken in, say, twenty years' time.

The earliest impressions of a stranger upon entering the control room of a modern signal box might well be first of quiet and calm, and then of the surprising beauty of the scene. Here is none of the clamour of a big old-style mechanical box, with its incessant ringing of the block bells, the clang of heavy levers, and the occasional flinging open of the windows for a message to be shouted through the megaphone. Instead one finds a pleasant spacious room, with diffused lighting, a parquet floor,

121

and the few signalmen operating points and signals, that may be anything up to a couple of miles distant, by moving miniature chromium-plated levers. Add to this the gay colours of the track diagrams, and the hundreds of coloured lights, displayed on the panel behind the levers and constantly changing in synchronism with the reds, yellows and greens displayed by the colour-light signals out on the line—the visitor may well stand awhile, fascinated, before he begins to take in some details of the equipment.

Mounted on a shelf in front of the levers are bronze plates describing the signals or points concerned. One reads titles like "No. 2 Platform Starter to Down Main", and beneath the description are varying numbers of figures; these latter give what are termed the "pulls", in other words the other levers in the machine which must be pulled over before the particular one is released by the interlocking. But one rarely sees an experienced signalman refer to the designation plates at all; these men appear to know instinctively the whereabouts of the combinations they require. The interlocking between levers is entirely electric, and the visitor can see for himself, through glass panels extending to the floor, the contacts through the agency of which the circuits are made or broken. It is always interesting to watch the actual coming and going of trains as depicted by the lighting and extinguishing of lamps on the illuminated track diagram. These lights are controlled by track circuits, in which current is normally flowing in the rails but is cut off during the passage of a train.

The introduction of electric interlocking has made possible the latest developments in control machines, wherein the miniature lever has been replaced in some cases by a small thumb switch and in others by a push button. After some early installations in years just before World War II which can now be regarded as experimental, the principle of route switching has been generally adopted, and all work done in connexion with the Modernization Plan of British Railways at the larger centres has been based upon the use of control consoles of the most advanced design. Instead of having separate levers for each signal and each pair of points a complete route is set up in some systems by the operation of only two push buttons, and in another by turning of a single thumb switch. The larger the area that can be brought under the control of one signal box the better will be the regulation of traffic, and much ingenuity has been displayed in miniaturization of these modern control machines, so as to minimize the amount of walking about the men themselves have to do, and in presenting them with the widest possible "picture" of traffic movements in the most compact space on their illuminated diagram.

Since the very early days of railways elaborate precautions have been taken to prevent signalmen making mistakes; they, however, represent only one side of railway operating. The utmost refinements of interlocking would be of no avail if enginemen could not see the signals. Nowadays much care is spent in choosing the location and the height of the signals, so as to give an unobstructed view to the driver, and in ordinary circumstances no difficulty is experienced on the footplate. It is when an engine is in trouble, or the weather is thick that mistakes are most likely to be made. There is the tragic example of the Aisgill collision, on the Midland, in the autumn of 1913. On the heavy gradients between Appleby and the summit of the line the engine of a southbound train was steaming badly; an injector failed, and the driver so busied himself in putting this right and in supervising his fireman's efforts that he misread an important signal, and went on to crash into the rear of another train.

It is to guard against such errors that various systems of automatic train control have been devised. That used over the whole main line network of the Great Western Railway has proved most effective in service, and from personal experience on the footplate I can testify to the feeling of complete confidence that it gives. The working can be explained by description of a typical ten minutes in the cab. You are tearing down the incline from Whiteball Tunnel: the engine is tossing a little as she takes one reverse curve after another, and so we bear down upon the "distant" signal for Wellington. The fireman who has been looking ahead shouts "right away" —we are signalled through Wellington and into the next block section. But just before we pass the signal itself we run over a ramp placed between the rails, and simultaneously we get a short but loud ring on the electric bell in the cab; that is the confirming cab signal that we are "right away". So we sweep on, 70 m.p.h., and faster still, on a splendid piece of road, till nearing Taunton; then, some distance ahead an adverse signal is sighted, and the driver shuts off steam. But it might not have been so easy to see that signal in mist, or driving rain. As before, we come to the ramp; but this time, as we pass over, a little horn on the side of the cab starts up in a blood-curdling imitation of an air-raid siren. The driver stops it at once by operating a lever; otherwise the piercing note would continue and the brakes would be applied.

Since nationalization the principle of the Automatic Warning System, as it is now termed, has been applied to other British main lines, with the difference that the "pick-up" is inductive, instead of through a contact ramp. Behind all the work in the signal boxes, and the running of the trains themselves, are the District and Divisional Controls. There was a time when the dispatch of goods trains from important centres of traffic was quite haphazard. Local superintendents, anxious to get rid of the coal, merchandise, or whatever it was, sent off train after train regardless of how the line was already occupied, or how the receiving centres were situated for handling the traffic. The result often was hopeless congestion. In working the coal traffic from South Yorkshire the Midland Railway was sometimes so completely blocked that engine crews booking off for a period of rest returned many hours later to take over the same train, which had not turned a wheel in the meantime.

It was the late Sir Cecil Paget who, when General Superintendent of the Midland Railway, laid the foundations of modern British railway operation by the introduction of a control system for freight train working. The keynote of this system was a strict regulation of all movements, so that heavy goods trains would not only get a clear path when out on the road, but also would not have to wait when they came to the marshalling yards. Apart from the experimental control installed at Masborough in 1907 the first section to be brought under the new system was that between Cudworth and the marshalling yards at Toton, near Nottingham. It was later extended to cover the whole of the Midland Railway system, and to include passenger trains as well. Nowadays it is the generally accepted scheme of operation throughout the country.

The telephone is the basis of the whole scheme. Every morning the Divisional Controller holds a telephone conference with each of his District Controllers, so that Headquarters is acquainted with the general traffic situation throughout the length and breadth of the system. Signalmen at key points report by telephone to District Control the time at which all trains pass their box. Passenger stations report the loading of the principal express trains, so that Divisional Control can, if necessary, arrange for extra coaches to be added and assistant engines provided when needed. A District Control may report a glut of freight traffic; Divisional Control thereupon arrange for special trains to clear it, and if the reception areas cannot take it at once intermediate accommodation must be found. The essence of the whole scheme is to keep a constant watch on train movements, on the principle that the only way to deal with congestion is never to let it occur.

Paget certainly ranks among the greatest figures in British railway history. Trained as a mechanical engineer he rose to the position of Assistant Locomotive Superintendent of the Midland Railway. Then, at the

early age of 33, he was appointed General Superintendent, and began that short, though brilliant tenure of the
office by which his name will always be honoured among
railwaymen. It was characteristic of him not merely to
visit the most congested sections of the Midland Railway; he lived in an inspection coach on the spot, watch-
ing the working night and day, and gradually he formu-
lated the scheme of traffic control which is nowadays so
widely used. It was during this period of "caravan" life
that his qualities as an epicure and chef became known.
As in France, during his equally brilliant command of
the Railway Operating Division in the war of 1914–
1918, he did all his own cooking. It was one of the
tragedies of the post-1918 period that his fine leadership
and exceptional talent for organization were lost to the
British railways; for he retired at the early age of 44,
and entered the field of commerce.

4

Then and Now

AN otherwise ordinary morning in late June, 1938, brought a surprising invitation from the Information Agent of the London and North Eastern Railway. "I wonder if I can persuade you," his letter began, "to come for a run down the line next Tuesday afternoon." Then, after telling me what was afoot he finished by asking me to treat the news I had been given as strictly confidential for the time being. I needed no persuasion to join that little excursion party, and it was in anticipation of a unique experience that I presented my credentials at King's Cross on the appointed afternoon. The year, as I have said, was 1938, and the period just fifty years since the age-old rivalry between the East and West Coast routes to Scotland had blazed up into the first "Race to the North".

This modern occasion was the first public appearance of some new rolling stock for the "Flying Scotsman", some of the finest this country has ever seen; but in introducing this stock the L.N.E.R. staged a pleasing piece of railway pageantry. The luxurious new train by which we were to travel to Grantham was nowhere in evidence at King's Cross; instead, to the astonishment of the usual lunch-hour platform-strollers, was drawn up a replica of the train of 1888: seven trim little six-wheeled-coaches, lighted with oil lamps, and having no corridors and no restaurant car. Early arrivals among the Company's guests had hardly begun to take in the details of this fascinating museum piece when the engine came backing down, the sole survivor of Patrick Stirling's famous eight-foot single wheelers, long since retired from active service and ordinarily kept in the Railway Museum at York.

To the locomotive we were instantly drawn by the flashy array of polished brass and copper work; by the huge single pair of driving wheels, the slotted splasher, and the height of the chimney. Then, quite apart from any technical features, one appraised straightway the perfect balance and symmetry of the external lines. Someone on the platform remarked: "What an artist Stirling must have been!" Another guest whose mind was evidently running on more practical lines was overheard saying to a friend, "I hope the boiler doesn't burst!" For that highly embellished old veteran had got to work that afternoon, and work reasonably hard. We were to travel to Stevenage in the old train, and there to transfer into the new "Flying Scotsman". Before the start one formed the impression that fifty years ago most, if not all the designer's decorative skill was bestowed upon the engine; while the carriage exteriors were smartly finished and carried the East Coast Joint Stock coat of arms, beautifully rendered, the interior of the compartments were so severely plain as to recall instinctively the earliest railway days when passengers travelled in vehicles little removed from open boxes.

King's Cross is not the easiest station from which to start away on a brisk run; after threading the maze of points and crossings at the platform end the line begins to rise steeply, at 1 in 105, and what is more through a tunnel. For this reason it can be particularly awkward to a "single-driver" locomotive which has only the weight borne by the one driving axle to provide the adhesion. But the driver had evidently been well schooled in the art of handling her, for he got the train away without a sign of slipping, and took us up the long climb to Potters Bar at a galloping 50 m.p.h. The riding of the six-wheeled coaches brought forth much amusing comment; one missed the buoyant swing of a modern bogie coach, and felt a sense of fussing and bustling along. After we passed over the crest of the bank at Potters Bar the gallant old engine was taken under easy steam for the rest of the journey, and no attempt was made to repeat the high speed performance that this class of engine used regularly to put up in its prime. So we came to Stevenage, and found the new train waiting to take us on to Grantham.

Stepping straight from the replica of 1888, we were at once confronted with the immense change that has taken place in railway travel in the past fifty years. Between one of those old first-class non-corridor compartments, and the cosy interior of a stage coach there is little difference in principle; but the compartments of the new train, which, of course, were corridor throughout, were each more like little private drawing-rooms, each decorated in exquisite taste—beautiful coloured etchings on the walls, a profusion of mirrors, a carpet on the floor, and

130

one spacious window, instead of the opening door and its modest adjoining peepholes. In external appearance the new train was obviously a true lineal descendant of the veteran in which we had travelled down from London. There was the same varnished teak finish. No less contrasting than the carriage interiors, however, were the locomotives. At the head of the new train was a great blue streamlined Pacific, that one indeed that bears the honoured name of the designer *Sir Nigel Gresley*. But apart from the bizarre effect of its sweeping curves and shrouding one could not help remarking upon the extreme plainness of the finish. Vivid and strikingly-coloured though this modern engine might be she was every inch a utility job, designed to be serviced and cleaned in the minimum possible time.

On the run north that day we were very soon treated to a remarkable exposition of the new standards of long-distance passenger train running that had been set up before the outbreak of war. It was not so much that the weight of locomotives and rolling stock had increased, but that the whole standard of speed had been raised. At the time of the 1888 Race to Scotland, and indeed for quite forty years afterwards the generally accepted standard of speed for an express train on level track was 60 m.p.h.; one travelled a good deal slower up the banks, and up to 75 and sometimes 80 m.p.h. downhill, but a mile a minute on the flat was the basic speed of travel. Yet on this memorable afternoon our streamlined Pacific took the new "Flying Scotsman" train tearing northward at speeds of 86 and 87 m.p.h. sustained on level track. And this was not with a special lightweight train; our load was no less than fourteen of the heaviest and most luxurious coaches this country has ever seen. Although undeniably a specially fast run was made for exhibition purposes, the general standard of running with these very heavy trains is between 70 and 75 m.p.h. on level track. As to maximum speeds, less than a week later one of the same class of locomotive, named *Mallard*, secured for Britain the world's record with steam haulage, by attaining 126 m.p.h. in the course of a special test run. Patrick Stirling's single-wheelers rarely used to exceed about 75 m.p.h. in ordinary service, and the most that has been recorded with them is 85 m.p.h.

On the other hand their great rivals, the little "Precedents" of the London and North Western Railway, used to knock up some terrific speeds when running downhill from Shap. "Eighties" were common, and there were cases when they got up to 87 and 88 m.p.h. Studying their slender proportions, and recalling too that they weighed but 33 tons, the question naturally arises as to what it was like riding on them at such speeds. An engine-man of another railway, writing under the pen-name of "L.B.S.C.", has described in vivid terms such an experience between Rugby and Willesden, on a locomotive named *The Auditor*: "There was a most appalling clatter as we tore through the junction at Bletchley, but no pitching nor tossing, she rode just like the Brighton six-wheeled engines, quite steady on the open road, but with a slight 'galloping' movement through points and crossings. I gave the fireman a few minutes' rest between Bletchley and Leighton, then we came to the long bank up to Tring. It was now dark, and old *Auditor* going all

132

out up Tring cutting was a sight I shall ever remember—
the top of the chimney looked like what I should imagine
Mount Vesuvius looked like in the last days of Pompeii.
Red, orange, and blue flames and millions of sparks and
red-hot lumps; honestly, I believe a Brighton 'Terrier'
could have run on what she threw away. The firehole
was just like an electric arc-lamp; how the firebars stayed
put, instead of melting up, was a marvel; but the old
cat absolutely seemed to enjoy it. . . ."

Not so many years ago I did have an opportunity of
riding upon a very similar contemporary of these
L.N.W.R. "Precedents"—at nearly 70 m.p.h. Some
older engines on which I have ridden become violently
rough at speed; the rear end crashes from side to side,
and the footplate is soon ankle-deep in coal. This little
engine however developed a peculiar bouncing action,
and the moment we struck the slightest curve in the track
she set up a hearty corkscrew roll in addition. One rarely
notes such curious antics with large modern locomotives,
unless they are nearly due for general repairs. They ride
very hard, due of course to the high concentration of
weight in a short space, but usually they are steady
enough, even at speeds of 80 m.p.h. From this glimpse
of railway travel fifty years ago with its many contrasts
to the conditions of today, it is only natural to dig still
deeper into railway history.

The riding qualities of locomotives were a matter of
serious concern to the engineers of a hundred years ago;
as the size of boilers and the diameter of driving wheels
increased there was a general feeling that the gradual
raising of the centre of gravity was rendering engines un-

safe, and more and more liable to overturn when rounding curves. Steadiness was one of the trump cards of the Great Western, with their seven-foot gauge, but was singular indeed that one narrow-gauge "solution" to the difficulty should have come from an engineer who had served under the elder Brunel. It was in 1843 that Thomas Crampton patented his famous design for a single-driver express locomotive with the driving axle behind the boiler back-plate. By this means he was able to fit an unusually large boiler, and at the same time keep it down low, since its height was unaffected by the level of the driving axle.

But while Crampton may have achieved stability, he did so at the expense of the riding, which was harsh and subject to extreme vibration on the footplate. In striking contrast McConnell's tall express engines on the London and Birmingham with a decidedly high centre of gravity, had a beautifully easy action. Crampton's locomotives were never looked upon with any great favour in this country, but they became very popular in France, particularly on the Northern and Eastern Railways, so much so that their designer's name grew to be synonymous with railway travel itself. *Prendre le Crampton* was for a time a common term meaning travel by train. One of his finest engines *Le Continent* is preserved not in his native country but at the Gare de l'Est in Paris.

In May 1892 there came to an end the picturesque episode of the broad gauge on the Great Western Railway. For many years it provided one of the strongest links with the earliest days of railways. Owing to the impending change to the standard gauge little was done in the later years to modernize broad gauge equipment, and a journey to the West of England by G.W.R. was in many ways a novel experience. The death-knell of the broad gauge, of Brunel's magnificent conception of a high speed railroad, was sounded in 1846, when the findings of the Royal Commission upon the gauge question was confirmed by Act of Parliament. Henceforth no further extension of the broad gauge would be sanctioned. The opposition certainly was overwhelming. At the time the Commission sat the Great Western had 270 miles of broad gauge lines, whereas in other parts of the country there were no less than 1,900 miles of narrow gauge.

The protagonists of the broad gauge would appear to have been fighting a losing battle from the outset on this score alone; but Brunel himself was so thoroughly confident in the technical superiority of the broad gauge that he sincerely hoped to reverse the seemingly inevitable decision and secure the conversion of all existing British railways to the seven-foot gauge. What such a decision would have involved, financially, did not seem to deter Brunel. In his view the narrow gauge was not the best, and therefore it was not to be considered! To him the possibilities for high speed were the main criteria by which any railway should be judged. He was intolerant of any other point of view. In 1838 he wrote: "I shall not attempt to argue with those who consider any increase in speed unnecessary. The public will always prefer that conveyance which is the most perfect; and speed, within reasonable limits, is a material ingredient in perfection of travelling."

By the year 1848, as if to cast the decision of the Royal Commission back in their teeth, the Great Western had developed some sensationally fast trains. The morning mail train was booked to cover the 53 miles from Paddington to Didcot in 56 minutes, start to stop, a speed that none of the narrow gauge companies could approach at that time. This high speed later earned for the train its nickname of The Flying Dutchman, after the Derby and St. Leger winner of 1849. How the carriages of that period travelled at such speeds is not recorded, but in any case there would be some on board the trains who would be glad to get the journey over as soon as possible. The old third-class compartments seated no less than seven a side, and were narrow into the bargain, with very little room for the knees. The coach builders were not very generous with window space either, and it is to be feared that the passengers unfortunate enough to have the middle seats on each side saw precious little of the countryside on these journeys to and from the west.

Those who could see out would notice Brunel's peculiar form of permanent way. It was then usual for the rails to be supported on stone blocks, spaced at regular intervals, the blocks preceding the use of the timber sleepers so familiar to-day. In building the Great Western Railway Brunel used what was termed a bridge rail, supported by continuous longitudinal timbers. Unlike those of the Stephensons Brunel's rails had continuous support underneath, and were made considerably lighter in consequence. In quest of increased stability for his road Brunel supported the joints in the timbers upon piles driven from seven to ten feet deep into the ground.

But this very rigidity proved a cause of much unsatisfactory riding of the trains, and led to an agitation for Brunel's dismissal from the post of Engineer to the Company. At this crisis in the affairs of the Great Western two of his staunchest supporters among the directors took a trip on the London and Birmingham Railway in order to sample the riding of the coaches. This line had only recently been built by Robert Stephenson, and the rails were laid on stone blocks. Brunel's friends were delighted to find the riding as rough as on their own line, with frequent bumps and jolts, and a general sense of discomfort.

The piles had to go however, though the longitudinal timbers remained to the very end of the broad gauge. Ironically enough this type of permanent way lent itself far more readily to the alteration of the gauge, when the time came, than the orthodox transverse-sleepered road would have done. Even after the piles had been removed its inherent stiffness remained a handicap to easy running, and after the conversion of the gauge when some parts of the line had been relaid, while others retained the longitudinals, experienced enginemen averred that their locomotives would pull a considerably heavier load on the new track. Today, pieces of the old ";bridge" rails may be seen doing humble duty as girders or stays in many a building in the West Country.

Associated with the Great Western was the South Devon Railway, running from Exeter to Plymouth. Here, difficulties of the terrain afforded ample scope for Brunel's imaginative genius. He secured a perfectly level route from Exeter as far as Newton Abbot by carrying the railway along the base of the red sandstone cliffs from Dawlish to Teignmouth; and along this picturesque stretch of line, which invariably brings crowds of passengers to the corridor windows of modern holiday expresses, he tried out one of the most daring and least successful of his many innovations. The line beyond Newton Abbot, carried across the foothills of Dartmoor, was extremely hilly, so much so that it was considered impracticable to use locomotives of ordinary design. Brunel, ever ready to try out a novelty, recommended the use of what was termed the "atmospheric" system of propulsion.

The system, which was already installed on a short length of coastal railway in Ireland, required no locomotives as such. The trains were coupled to a small four-wheeled carriage from which was suspended a piston; this piston worked in a continuous pipe fifteen inches in diameter and laid between the rails. The air from this pipe was pumped out by stationary engines fixed at intervals along the line, and the suction thus created in front of the piston was sufficient to haul the train along. The scheme has a fantastic ring about it; but it worked, and speeds up to 70 m.p.h. were attained!

The trouble in actual practice arose from the need for making provision for the connexion between the piston and the carriage. The pipe had a continuous slot at the top, which slot was normally sealed by a leather flap. An arrangement of wheels pushed up the flap to allow the piston connexion to pass, after which it was resealed. It is easy to be wise after the event, but nowadays the idea of that flap does not strike one as a sound engineer-

138

ing proposition. The constant passage of trains and the pushing aside of the leather would seem to invite excessive wear and tear, and of course once leakage began the railway might just as well close down! Nevertheless the system was duly installed from Exeter as far as Newton Abbot, and it worked well at first. Passengers were delighted by the smoothness of the running, and by the absence of all smoke and dirt.

But long before wear and tear of passing trains could affect the leather, rats and the sea air had taken their toll; leakage increased in the pipe at times to such an extent that a vacuum could not be created sufficient to haul the trains, and traffic was brought to a standstill. By dint of constant vigilance, frequent repairs, and even complete renewal of the leather throughout the pipe line traffic was kept going, after a fashion, between Exeter and Newton Abbot; but after a mere eight months' service Brunel was compelled to admit failure, to advise the scrapping of the entire atmospheric system, and the substitution of steam locomotives. This disastrous misjudgment cost the company nearly half a million pounds, while Brunel lost heavily himself, having, as always, invested substantially in any project he was installing.

On the South Devon line, and also farther west on the Cornwall Railway, there stood for some time a far nobler series of monuments to Brunel's genius than the useless, pathetic engine houses of the atmospheric system. In carrying the railway across the numerous deep valleys and tidal creeks he adopted a most picturesque design of timber trestle viaduct. There were numerous varieties of this broad general design, some of which were built on stone piers, and others in which the legs were wholly of timber. The latter were used in crossing the tidal creeks between Devonport and St. Germans. In places the mud reaches a depth of 70 feet and the piles driven down to a solid foundation were made of such a length that their upward ends formed the supports for the bridge girders. The Cornwall Railway was originally built as a single line, and when doubling became necessary the old viaducts were replaced generally by masonry arched structures.

Several of the finest examples of Brunel's trestle viaducts survived on the Falmouth branch until 1931. It was an unusual experience to ride over these viaducts, for even those carried on stone piers used to sway gently with the passage of the trains. Some of the structures as actually constructed were bold enough, such as St. Pinnock, with a height of 150 feet above the valley, or Truro, with a length of nearly 1,300 feet; but even these would have been altogether eclipsed had Brunel's original proposal for crossing the Tamar been accepted by the Admiralty. His first design was for a timber viaduct having a central span of 250 feet, and six smaller spans of 100 feet, affording a clear headway of 70 feet above high water mark. It would have been a magnificent specimen of timber viaduct; but the Admiralty demanded a bridge having four spans of 300 feet, two of 200 feet, and a clear headway of 100 feet, and in face of these requirements Brunel abandoned the idea of using timber, instead producing his superb wrought iron bridge described in the second chapter of this book.

The inability of early locomotives to climb steep

gradients led to the adoption of cable traction for certain short lengths of line. On the London and Birmingham Railway a splendidly graded route was built, save in the immediate approach to Euston, where the Regents canal had to be crossed only a short distance from the terminus. Between the canal bridge and the station the gradient was between 1 in 70 and 1 in 112 for nearly a mile, and when the railway was first opened, locomotive haulage ceased at Chalk Farm. Northbound trains were pushed by hand to the end of the departure platform; the leading carriage was then attached to an endless rope, and the train hauled up to the top of the incline by two powerful stationary winding engines. At Euston this method of operation was in use for only six years, and in 1844 locomotives began working the trains throughout to Birmingham. The Camden incline is not unduly steep however, and once the steam locomotive had been developed into a sound working proposition it was found that any efficient type of engine could take its maximum running load up the incline without assistance.

The L.M.S Pacific engines used to take 15 and 16 coach trains out of Euston unaided. Some trains it is true have a "pusher" engine in rear, but this is merely a matter of operational convenience. The empty stock for certain long-distance expresses is housed in the carriage sheds just outside Euston; these are backed into the station by a yard engine, and when loaded taken up the Camden incline by the main line engine alone. Other trains are brought into the terminus from carriage sheds at Willesden, and these of course, have to be drawn into the station. The locomotive which has brought in the empty stock is already available at the rear of the train when the journey proper is begun, and its services are used to give the main line engine some assistance up the bank.

On another famous incline where cable haulage was used, that from Queen Street Station, Glasgow, on the former North British Railway, the gradient was altogether more severe. The Cowlairs incline, as it is known, is 1¼ miles long, with a slope of 1 in 45, and here cable traction was used until 1908. To avoid the need for stopping at the summit the main line locomotive was attached to the train at the terminus, and this locomotive was connected to the endless cable by what was termed a messenger rope. On the buffer beam of the locomotive there was a special inverted hook to which the messenger rope was attached. When the train reached the summit of the incline and began to accelerate, the winding engine was stopped, and the messenger rope dropped clear of the hook so that the train could go straight ahead without stopping.

The Cowlairs incline formed part of the Edinburgh and Glasgow Railway, which was opened in 1842. On most of the early railways traffic came fairly easily. The public were attracted by the new form of travel, and indeed some lines, the Liverpool and Manchester for example, had such a spate of passenger traffic that the conveyance of merchandise was for a time a secondary consideration. It was far otherwise however in the case of the Edinburgh and Glasgow. From the very outset this railway was up against the Forth and Clyde Canal Company. Apart from the Cowlairs incline the new railway

142

had been built on an almost level course, remarkable indeed, considering the hilly nature of the country traversed; but from the inception of the line the possibilities for high speed were never developed.

Had the railway introduced trains running at no more than 30 m.p.h. the canal people would not have stood a chance; the railway affairs were however so bungled that the canal was not only able to retain a goodly proportion of the freight traffic, but also to enter into serious competition for the passenger business as well! It was then that the famous "fly boats" were introduced, specially light craft which were drawn by a team of two, or sometimes three horses, and run at the "express" speed of 7 to 8 m.p.h. Railway and Canal then entered into a cut-throat competition in fares. In 1845 one could travel from Edinburgh to Glasgow by the Swift Passage Boats, at these were called, for 1s. 4d., while by the night boats the steerage fare was only 1s. 0d. The railway, instead of replying with increased speed, reduced their fares, whereupon the canal people regaled their passengers with band performances while they waited at the termini, and gave away refreshments *en route*! This followed the startling precedent set by the rival Irish boat services from the Clyde, which at the zenith of their equally absurd competition for traffic presented every passenger with a bottle of beer! Ultimately the single fare from Edinburgh to Glasgow by both railway and canal was reduced to 6d., after which the railway company at last took the initiative and bought up the canal.

Musical accompaniments seem to have been quite a favourite stock-in-trade of early railway operators. On

143

the London and Greenwich Railway bands played the trains in and out at both termini. This practice has its modern counterpart in the music broadcast at intervals on the loudspeakers at Waterloo, Southern Region. As the first railway in London, the Greenwich line received perhaps more than its fair shair of publicity, both favourable and adverse. In certain quarters it was usual for the slightest mishap to be magnified out of all proportion, and those who did venture to travel were written down as "noodles". With those of a more adventurous turn of mind it became the fashion to make up railway "parties", to travel to and from Greenwich, for example, just for the experience. Lady Hardy acted as hostess on one such occasion though she could not persuade her spouse, Nelson's gallant flag-captain at Trafalgar, to take the "risk", and join the party.

The risks associated with early railway travel became a matter for national concern in 1842 when Queen Victoria made her first journey by rail. One newspaper went so far as to say: "A long regency in this country would be so fearful and tremendous an evil that we cannot but desire, in common with many others, that those Royal railway excursions should be, if possible, either wholly abandoned, or only occasionally resorted to." This first journey was from Slough to Paddington, by the Great Western. As befitted so momentous an occasion Daniel Gooch, the Locomotive Superintendent, himself drove the engine, and Brunel rode with him on the footplate. The Queen, far from showing any apprehension, wrote afterwards that she was quite charmed with the experience. A year before this Lady Holland, then 71

25 Testing a locomotive at Swindon: the "King Edward VII" anchored on the stationary plant, running at an equivalent road speed of 75 m.p.h., and developing 2000 horsepower

26 Old style signal box at Bishop's Stortford, Essex

27 The huge new signal box at Wilmslow, Cheshire, on the electrified
Crewe–Manchester line

28 Old style signal gantry (now removed) in the southern approach to York

29 Colour light signals on the electrified line outside Manchester Piccadilly

30 Renewal of the formation on one of Britain's oldest main lines: at Denbigh Hall, near Bletchley, two of the four tracks are out of use while sand is being off-loaded and spread to form the basis of the renewed road-bed

31 The new Wood-
head Tunnel,
Manchester – Sheffield
line: travelling steel
shutter assembled ready
for boring the new
double-line tunnel

32 Highland express locomotive, "Strathnairn" of 1892, designed by David Jones

SCOTTISH LOCOMOTIVES OF THE NINETIES

33 Glasgow and South Western, 4–4–0 of 1892 design, by James Manson

34 A 2000 h.p. Diesel-electric hauling the up "Merseyside Express",
Liverpool to Euston, near Watford, Herts

DIESEL HAULED EXPRESSES

35 A Diesel-hydraulic, D.601 "Ark Royal", on the "Cornish Riviera
Express" near Reading, Berks

36 The Doric Arch at Euston, built 1838, now in course of demolition to make room for the enlargement and modernisation of the station

STATION EXTERIORS OLD AND NEW

37 The new exterior at Crewe, Cheshire, completed 1961

years of age, braved the journey from Paddington to Chippenham in order to visit Lord Lansdowne, her husband's cousin. She contrived however to make the journey in the company of Brunel himself, and for greater safety insisted upon holding his hand all the way!

It was only natural that ordinary folk found speeds of 30 m.p.h. or so alarming after previously experiencing nothing swifter than a stage coach. But with the increase in power of steam locomotives both permanent way and coaching stock improved, so that the attainment of higher speeds synchronised with a growth of railway-mindedness in the country in general, and mile-a-minute travel was accepted as a natural rather than a sensational development. With increasing speeds, and with the increasing weight of locomotives and coaches there crept little by little into railway operation a danger that does not seem to have been fully appreciated by the responsible officers, and which was certainly unheeded by the public: brake power was not being developed on a scale commensurate with the rapid advance in the tractive and speed capabilities of the locomotives.

The public were brought into violent realization of the primitive methods in use, as late at 1876, by the disastrous collision on the Great Northern Railway at Abbots Ripton. On the evening of January 21st that year a blizzard of exceptional severity was sweeping over eastern England; wires were down, signals were frozen, and owing to some signals displaying a false clear indication the southbound "Flying Scotsman" collided with a coal train at Abbots Ripton sidings, some $4\frac{1}{2}$ miles north of Huntingdon. But that unfortunately was not all. At the time of the first crash an express from London to Leeds had already passed Huntingdon, and was actually passing Stukeley signal box when the man on duty there received news from Abbots Ripton that the line was blocked. He could do nothing to warn the northbound express. The first of the Abbots Ripton signals, the distant, was over 1,000 yards from the scene of the smash, but that signal too was frozen in the clear position, and the driver of the express sighting it through the driving snow, continued at full speed, thinking that the line was clear.

The one piece of good fortune in the whole affair was that the men of the coal train had, after the smash, uncoupled their engine and gone forward towards Huntingdon in order to fix detonators on the northbound line. They were just level with the distant signal when the express approached, and by repeated whistling and the display of a red lamp they managed to warn the driver. Although the train was travelling at barely 50 m.p.h., that distance of 1,000 yards proved insufficient in which to stop, and the Leeds express ploughed into the wreckage of the other two trains. The Leeds express consisted of thirteen four-wheeled coaches, but the only brake power available was that from two vans, hand operated by the guards, and the locomotive and tender brakes. Eleven of the coaches had no brakes at all, and the collision might have been worse still had not the driver reversed the engine to help matters.

It may seem regrettable that so much of our present railway operating system has been developed from the experience of fatal accidents; but it must be remembered that engineering science itself was only feeling its way, step by step, with railway development. Rule-of-thumb methods were far more popular than anything resembling a scientific approach. Yet for all that one can appraise the keen practical ability of some of the early rule-of-thumb designers. A few years ago a highly mathematical paper was read before one of the engineering institutions on the design of signal posts. In the subsequent discussion a veteran of the profession remarked that to him the main point about the paper was that it showed with what remarkable accuracy the men of sixty or seventy years ago had guessed the correct proportions for their posts.

Many operating principles that we should now consider risky seemed quite all right until some unexpected circumstance arose. The frozen signals at Abbots Ripton were a case in point. Until then it was usual for signals to be kept in the lowered, or all-clear position; they were raised to the danger position after the passage of a train, and lowered again after the train had passed the next signal box down the line. When trains were infrequent the signals remained in the clear position for long periods, and on that unfortunate night they became so weighted down and clogged by ice and snow that they could not be put to danger. As a result of that experience the system was changed so as to keep the signals normally at danger, and to lower them only when required for the passage of a train.

In the early days of railways various clever traffic manœuvres were used for the "slick" working of trains. So that locomotives need not enter terminal stations the following practice was tried: at a certain pre-arranged point approaching the terminus the locomotive was uncoupled; the driver then put on full steam and drew sufficiently far ahead for the locomotive to be switched into a siding and for the points to be reset in time to send the carriages gliding into the station. With skilful braking on the guard's part this arrangement worked very smoothly; but then, one day in 1840 a gentleman less expert, or perhaps less careful, piled his whole train into the buffers at Hull.

This proceeding has its counterpart in the modern practice of slipping coaches, in order to give a service to intermediate stations where long distance express trains do not stop. But it is not merely a matter of uncoupling the last coach, or coaches at the appropriate spot and allowing them to coast into the station. All passenger trains are now fitted with automatic continuous brakes, which in the event of a breakage of the couplings anywhere in the train automatically bring both portions to rest. The slip coach, or the first of a series being slipped, is fitted with a special valve for isolating it at the correct time from the brake system of the main part of the train, so that the uncoupling of the brakepipe preparatory to the releasing of the special slip drawbar does not bring the main part of the train to rest. At one time the practice of slipping coaches was extensively used in many parts of the country, on, among others, the London and North Western, Great Eastern and Great Central Railways, in addition to the largest user of all, the Great Western. The L.N.W.R. was the only line to slip corridor coaches; on all others passengers in the slip coaches had no access to restaurant cars, or other parts of the main train. But in 1939 only the Great Western was continuing this interesting procedure. At one period the "Cornish Riviera Express" carried no less than three slip portions: one detached at Westbury consisting of through carriages for the Weymouth line; a portion including carriages for Ilfracombe and Minehead slipped at Taunton; and finally a portion for Torquay and Kingswear, slipped at Exeter. Thus by this one departure from Paddington a very wide area of the West Country was served, although the main train made its first call as far west as Plymouth. The practice of slipping is now discontinued.

But while the braking of passenger trains is nowadays incomparably safer and more powerful than at the time of the Abbots Ripton collision no such improvement can be recorded so far as goods trains are concerned. It is true that a limited number of wagons have been equipped with continuous brakes, and that prior to the outbreak of war in 1939 some very fine express goods services were operated. But a high proportion in Great Britain still have the old loose couplings, and rely for their brake power solely upon the locomotive and a single guard's van. While this state of affairs continues the speed of the ordinary goods train must necessarily be slow, for any attempt at speeding would render the train completely out of control. The modern 80-wagon coal trains of the London and North Eastern Railway, representing a total weight of some 1,300 tons behind the tender, were nevertheless impressive modern descendants of the horse-drawn trains by which coal from Durham collieries was first conveyed over the metals of the Stockton and Darlington Railway.

When operation was first begun, each horse, harnessed to a train of four trucks, covered an average distance of 174 miles a week. Then the dandy carts were introduced. In travelling from the coalfield to the quayside at Stockton the railway was frequently on a falling gradient where the trucks, if solely under the influence of gravity, would travel considerably faster than if drawn by a horse. When a dandy cart was included in the train, the horse was detached at the top of each descent and led into the dandy whereupon the whole cavalcade tobogganed downhill at top speed. When the level track was reached and speed slackened off the horse resumed pulling. In this way the weekly mileage of the horses was increased from 174 to 240, and according to contemporary observers the animals seemed thoroughly to enjoy their rides in the dandy. The horses grew to know the points where they mounted the dandy cart, so much so that on occasions when, for some reason or other, the vehicle was not running, they ceased haulage as usual and attempted to get into the ordinary coal wagons. On the Stockton and Darlington Railway the dandy carts were used up to 1856.

The horse-drawn passenger coaches used when the Stockton and Darlington Railway was first opened in 1825 each carried fifteen passengers outside and three inside. Over the 12 mile journey speed averaged 10 m.p.h., with a maximum speed of 14 m.p.h. Each coach was drawn by a single horse, which made a double journey every day. Yet the coach ran so freely on the rails that it needed scarcely any exertion to maintain this relatively high speed. An early traveller records that in his experience it was only occasionally that the horse gave the vehicle a pull; at other times even in ascending from Stockton to Darlington the traces seemed to hang quite loose, and by far the greatest exertion of the horse appeared to consist in keeping up its own motion.

The use of horses for the haulage of passenger coaches enjoyed an amusing revival in the year of grace 1922, on none other than the Great Western Railway. In that year the evening non-stop express from Bristol to Paddington was scheduled to slip a coach at Swindon; to avoid the need for the main train to slow down, which would have been imperative if the slip coach had been detached on the platform road, slipping took place on the centre road, and the slip coach, which had travelled up from Bristol at modern express speed, was towed quietly into the platform by a horse!

At the time of the Abbots Ripton collision signalling arrangements were in what may be termed an intermediate state. The growth of traffic, the increase of speed, and the fact that the path of a train at a junction is out of the driver's control, all made it necessary to give the driver information as early as possible as to the state of the road ahead. In the earliest days it was usual for traffic to be controlled by "policemen" stationed at intervals along the line. Instructions to stop or proceed were given to the drivers of trains by hand signals in the day time and by lamps at night. From the work of these pioneer railway traffic policemen grew the whole art of signalling,

151

and to this day one often hears the signalman called "The Bobby".

At Junctions the policeman, picturesquely dressed in a tall hat and frock coat, also worked the points. As the speed of trains increased the hand signals could not be seen from a sufficient distance for the driver to take appropriate action, and so the human arm was replaced by a semaphore mounted on a tall post; the policeman operated the semaphore by a lever at the base of the post. The first step towards the now-universal practice of concentrating the control of signals and points at one place was made in 1843 by C. H., afterwards Sir Charles, Gregory, Engineer of the London and Croydon Railway. At Bricklayers Arms Junction, about two miles out of the terminus at London Bridge he arranged the controls for two pairs of points and four semaphore signals on a single platform, which, to give the policeman a better view up and down the line, was raised about six feet from the ground.

It is a far cry from this father of all signal boxes to a modern cabin like Northallerton, on the main line of the former L.N.E.R. Here it is not enough for the points and signals, some as much as two miles from the box, to be worked electrically. The work of the signalman is reduced to an absolute minimum by the use of the route system. In signalling a train through this busy junction the man has before him as a guide a diagrammatic representation on a large scale of all the running lines; referring to this he selects the route the train will follow and then turns the appropriate thumb switch. This single action automatically sets all the points on the route, and when they have all lined up correctly the signal changes from the "danger" to the "clear" position. Lastly as a final check, the route set up is illuminated as a series of white lights on the track diagram. The position of a train is indicated by red lights, and in actual practice it is thus rarely necessary, except when shunting operations are in progress, for the signalman so much as to look out of his cabin window. In operating these modern control machines it is remarkable how instinctive a touch is acquired by the men. After a very short time they seem to "feel" the whereabouts of the route switches they require with the skill of an experienced pianist.

As with the actual control of train movements, by means of the wayside signals, so equally in the sphere of traffic regulation has great progress been made. The work of the central Control has already been described, but it is not so many years ago that the whole business of regulation was left almost entirely to the discretion of individual signalmen. It was left to their judgement, or that of local stationmasters, to decide when a goods should be side tracked to make way for an express passenger, or mail train. Provided traffic flowed in fairly close accordance with the time table this arrangement worked satisfactorily, but the absence of some central directing authority was apt to lead to chaotic conditions once the workings got well out of gear.

But there were certain places where, even in normal circumstances, it would be asking too much of human nature to expect the old system to function smoothly. There was Red Hill, for example, on the main route from London to Brighton. North of that junction the line belonged to the South Eastern Railway and the London Brighton and South Coast exercised running powers for a distance of six miles northward to a junction called Stoat's Nest, near the site of the present station at Coulsdon. The signalman at Red Hill had a somewhat delicate task to perform, since he controlled the admission of South Eastern local trains from the Reading and Tonbridge directions to tracks also used by the Brighton main line expresses. The South Eastern certainly made things embarrassing for the Brighton people. The box at Red Hill was manned sometimes by a Brighton and sometimes by a South Eastern signalman, and each served his own company with a loyalty that often sadly discomfited the other party. The South Eastern men developed a simply uncanny skill for getting a train of empty coaches or a slow goods on to the main line just as a Brighton to London express was due. The Brightonians did their best in the way of counter-sabotage, but as the South Eastern ran nothing very important over their line the visitors had very much the worst of the deal. Matters eventually came to such a pass that the Brighton decided to build a new line of their own alongside the old one, on which they would at least have the track to themselves.

One very interesting feature of train working on the London, Brighton and South Coast Railway in Victorian times concerned the Continental service operated through the port of Newhaven. For some years this service was a tidal one, and since the departure time of the London-bound boat express was dependent upon the arrival time of the steamer the fitting in of suitable locomotive duties might well have been a very complicated process. To meet this difficulty the working was let by contract to one driver; the company provided a locomotive and the fuel, and the driver undertook to work the boat train to and from Newhaven at whatever time of the day or night it was required. He paid his own fireman and the shed cleaners. The locomotive concerned did no other work, and her modest mileage of 113 in the 24 hours is in striking contrast to the marathon turns operated in some present day locomotive "diagrams".

Not only in the Newhaven boat trains, but also on the regular Brighton main line workings each man had his own engine, and his name was duly painted in the cab. Nowadays a locomotive may be manned by eight different crews in the course of a single round of duties. In the summer of 1939 the L.N.E.R. was operating some very intricate "diagrams", as the rosters of duty are termed. The following is perhaps an extreme example, but is indicative of the measures introduced to get the greatest possible use out of the locomotive stock.

This round of duties was one of many worked by engines of the L.N.E.R. streamlined Pacific type stationed at King's Cross shed. With Doncaster men in charge the engine set out on a Monday with the 4 p.m. Newcastle express. At their home station the Doncaster crew were relieved by a second Doncaster crew, who took the train forward to York; there a North Eastern Area crew took over, and worked the train to Newcastle, where it arrived at 10.7 p.m. Then the engine had a short rest until about midnight, when a fresh North Eastern Area crew took charge preparatory to working the

"Aberdonian" sleeping car express at 1.14 a.m. non-stop from Newcastle to Edinburgh. The arrival in Edinburgh was at 3.50 a.m., after which the engine remained in charge of the same men for the return journey at 8.5 a.m. to Newcastle, arriving at 10.30 a.m. Having now covered 517 miles, all at express speed, in $18\frac{1}{2}$ hours, the engine was then given an off-spell for $9\frac{1}{2}$ hours, before working back to London, where the final arrival was at 3.15 a.m. On the homeward run the engine was triple-manned: a Gateshead crew as far as York, Peterborough men to Peterborough, and only on the final stage did men from the home shed, King's Cross, take charge.

A rather unfortunate result of this intensive working is that the time available between successive trains is much reduced; what time there is must necessarily be spent in essential servicing, and external cleanliness had, even before the war, become a secondary consideration. It may be argued that cleanliness does not matter so long as the locomotive does its work, but while the sight of one of these begrimed machines may not move the ordinary traveller to expressions of disgust, a gleaming, well-groomed engine will attract attention, and as such is a fine advertisement for the owning company. In the days when the old Brighton locomotive *Cardew* was working the Newhaven Continental boat trains, year in year out, engine cleaning was more of a ritual than a commercial proposition; enginemen took a great pride in the appearance of their locomotives, and even as recently as 1920 there was at least one driver, and a Scotsman at that, who used to give the cleaners a shilling a time to shine the buffers. The gay colours of nineteenth-

156

century British locomotives were in themselves an inducement to maintain a smart turnout.

The most striking of all these locomotive liveries of fifty years ago was undoubtedly that of the London, Brighton and South Coast Railway—a bright yellow, gorgeously set off by crimson under-frames, and a profusion of shining brass and copperwork. For some reason this colour was officially termed "improved engine green". Other distinctive colours were the royal blue of the Great Eastern, and the gamboge of the North British. The Caledonian provides perhaps the only instance of a railway changing, some forty years ago, from a relatively sombre to a gay livery. In the nineties the locomotives of this company were painted a dark blue, lined out in white; very handsome and dignified they looked. From about 1906 however, a gradual change was made to a bright sky blue, which in combination with purple underframes made one of the finest liveries ever seen on the British railways. It is strange to recall that this lighter blue colour came about quite unofficially. The painting was done by contract and the men bought the official dark blue from the company. White lead paint was however free, so the painters grew to work in as much of it as they dared, thus having to use less blue. The result was so attractive and so much admired that it came to be the recognised livery of the company. Some fine examples of nineteenth-century locomotives have fortunately been preserved, though not all of them are housed in places accessible to the public. Some are kept in the paint shop at Crewe works; the only example in Caledonian blue, together with a picturesque old Highland engine are similarly housed at St. Rollox Works, Glasgow.

Many famous steam locomotives have now been preserved, and in the expert hands of the British Transport Commission's Curator of Historical Relics they are displayed to excellent effect—some in the Railway Museum at York, and some in the Transport Museum at Triangle Place, Clapham. The engines of the northern lines, Great Northern, North Eastern, and the famous Brighton 0–4–2 *Gladstone* are at York, while engines of the south-country railways are at Clapham. Some beautiful examples of early Midland engines are kept in the old roundhouse at Derby, while others like the Great Western 4–4–0 *City of Truro*, scheduled as historical relics, are kept in full working order, and used for hauling special trains.

Alongside *Gladstone* in the York Museum there is a very ornate North Eastern express engine of 1875. Strange though it may seem the natural embellishments of this class, and of its contemporaries were not enough to satisfy the men, many of whom improved upon matters by adding large transfer pictures to the side of the sandbox, which was placed on the running plate just ahead of the driving wheels. All might have been well had these artistically-minded enginemen confined their attentions to members of the Royal Family, or statesmen; the latter suffered sometimes however if they happened to come within range of a cleaner of opposite political leanings, as when Mr. Gladstone, as depicted on a locomotive sandbox, emerged from a Leeds running shed with a black-eye. But one day a train from Thirsk came into Leeds hauled by a locomotive that quickly became the centre of a large and enthusiastic crowd. Examination of the sandbox disclosed not Disraeli, nor yet the Prince of Wales, but a classic goddess in diaphanous negligé! No wonder the passengers and staff at Leeds New station were thrilled; so was everyone else along the route from Leeds to Thirsk. Then, it is rumoured, the engine made a trip to York. Whether this alluring damsel was there spotted by some ecclesiastical dignitary and duly reported to Authority, or whether some headquarters' official of the North Eastern Railway took the matter into his own hands is not known; but in any event the lady vanished as swiftly as she had appeared.

It is greatly to be regretted that an example of one of the most distinctive of all nineteenth-century locomotive designs has not been preserved; I refer to the Webb three-cylinder compound type. Their designer, who for thirty years held the high office of Chief Mechanical Engineer on the London and North Western Railway, was one of those brilliant men who have left an indelible mark on British railway practice. He was imaginative, a first-rate organiser, and like Brunel most of his work was conceived on a big scale; but he was quite unapproachable—an autocrat, who would never listen to complaints—and while a great deal of his work was outstandingly successful, there is a strong probability that he was never fully aware of the extent of his failure. The three-cylinder compound engines were a case in point. They were provided with two pairs of driving wheels, but in order to combine the swiftness of a single-wheeler with the increased power to be derived from the two pairs of driving wheels, these two pairs were not coupled together. The leading pair were driven by the one low-pressure cylinder, while the other pair were driven by the two high-pressure cylinders.

Now if there is one feature that is absolutely essential in a compound engine it is perfect synchronization between the high and low pressure systems. The steam exhausted from the high-pressure cylinders should be assured of unrestricted flow to the low-pressure cylinder. This was to a certain extent achieved when running, but in starting, when all locomotives are liable to slip, the queerest things happened. The wheels driven by the high pressure cylinders would slip and send a volume of steam suddenly into the receiver, so that the whole system became choked; and if, as it might well happen, the ports of the low pressure cylinder were closed the engine would not start at all. The only thing to do was to open the cylinder drain cocks, and let out all the steam; then, reverse the engine, back a little—if she would move that way!—and so open the low pressure cylinder ports. Then you tried again, in forward gear.

So much time was wasted in coaxing these engines to start, that at one period it was actually a regular practice to employ men with pinchbars to get the compound-hauled trains away. Nevertheless they were handsome engines to look at, were beautifully kept, and in obedience to Webb's imperious orders put in a great deal of work on the crack trains. Unquestionably the most famous of them was No. 1304 *Jeanie Deans*. She belonged to what was known as the "Teutonic" class, which through certain modified features of their design were the most reliable, or perhaps I should say the least un-reliable, of the Webb three-cylinder compounds. *Jeanie Deans* for many years worked the afternoon Scottish express from Euston, one of the first all-corridor trains to run in this country; she went to Crewe on this job, returning in the evening with the corresponding south-bound train.

Although many more corridor trains were introduced on the L.N.W.R. the 2 p.m. from Euston was always known as "The Corridor" in the railway service. This name survived several changes in departure time, and even after the amalgamation, when the L.M.S officially named the train "The Midday Scot", it was still "The Corridor" to the staff. It was in July 1892 that the com-plete set of corridor coaches, with dining-car, began run-ning on this service between London and Glasgow, though Great Britain was distinctly behindhand in the introduction of corridors providing access from one com-partment to another. The Midland put into service in 1874 a train of cars built by the famous American de-signer George M. Pullman; in these vehicles communi-cation from one coach to the next was by way of open platforms at the ends.

The serving of meals in British trains actually pre-ceded, by a few years, the introduction of corridor stock as we know it today. The Great Northern Railway operated the first restaurant car, in 1879, between King's Cross and Leeds. This most ornate vehicle was again of American build, with clerestory roof, and open platforms at the ends that rendered it conspicuous among the rather undistinguished British rolling stock of that period. The whole scheme of decoration was at variance with that of our own severely plain carriage interiors; indeed modern taste would no doubt find the general air of affluence somewhat overpowering. Passengers were charged half-a-crown over and above the cost of their meal for the privilege of travelling in the car! The kitchen was fitted with a coke-burning range, and the scullery boy peeled the potatoes and did other menial tasks out on the open platform at the rear.

Prior to the introduction of dining-cars it was the practice with long distance trains to make special stops for meals at certain important intermediate stations. The "Flying Dutchman", of broad-gauge days on the Great Western stopped at Swindon for a luncheon interval of 20 minutes, and similar halts were made by the rival Anglo-Scottish expresses at Preston, Normanton and York respectively. But long before there were any trains running from England into Scotland, in fact in the very earliest days of main line travel a remarkably efficient refreshment-room had been established at Wolverton. This station then formed a kind of halfway house between London and Birmingham, and from 1840 onwards the express trains stopped for some ten minutes to enable passengers to sample the excellent fare available at all hours of the day or night.

But, as Sir Cusack Roney puts it in that extraordinary potpourri of his, *Rambles on Railways:*

". . . there was an attraction at those refreshment rooms that rose superior to all the hot soup, the hot coffee, the hot tea, the buns, the Banbury cakes, the pork pies, the brandy, whisky, gin, and 'rich compounds' . . . we refer to the charming young ladies in whom were concentred all the beauty and grace that should be corporated in modern Hebes."

And, in an extravagant eulogy of the virtues and chastity of these waitresses, he refers to

"sweet faces, worthy types of English beauty, all the more worthy because with them is combined the modest demeanour, emblem of purity, without which all is absent that adorns woman and renders her enchanting."

Another contemporary writer, Sir Francis Head, gives a most detailed description of the day's work in the Wolverton refreshment-rooms in his book *Stokers and Pokers*. Again the young ladies steal most of the limelight, though from his account in a manner well befitting their reputed maiden modesty. He writes:

"It is their rule, as well as their desire, never, if they can possibly prevent it, to speak to anyone; and although sometimes, when thunder has turned the milk, or the kitchen-maid over-peppered the soup, it may occasionally be necessary to soothe the fastidious complaints of some beardless ensign by an infinitesimal appeal to the generous feelings of his nature, we mean by the hundred-thousandth part of a smile, yet they endeavour on no account ever to exceed that harmless dose!"

163

Yet, somehow or other, nearly all those most exemplary of maidens managed to make excellent marriages.

When the London and Birmingham Railway was first opened throughout in 1838, the first-class trains were booked to make the journey of 112½ miles in five hours thirty-seven minutes, an average speed of 19 m.p.h. Of six daily trains four were run at this speed, while the slower variety took only half-an-hour longer. From the outset Sunday trains were run, though in many parts of the country similar proposals were met with terrific opposition from Sabbatarians. Not long after the opening of the Newcastle and Carlisle Railway the enterprising management advertised a day trip to Carlisle on a Sunday. Alongside the bills there appeared, as if by magic, another poster, which read:

"A reward for Sabbath Breaking. People taken safely and swiftly to Hell! Next Lord's Day, by the Carlisle Railway, for 7s. 6d. It is a pleasure trip!"

Sabbatarianism apart, the early railways had to face a great deal of opposition from those who stood out against the generally quickening tempo of life. Among these there was no more diehard opponent than John Ruskin. Apropos of the Derby and Manchester line he wrote:

"There was a rocky valley between Buxton and Bakewell, once upon a time divine as the Vale of Tempe; . . . You enterprised a railway through it —you blasted its rocks away. . . . The valley is gone and the Gods with it, and now every fool in Buxton

164

can be in Bakewell in half-an-hour and every fool in Bakewell at Buxton; which you think a lucrative progress of exchange—you fools everywhere."

Many years after his death the London and North Western, in naming a new series of express locomotives after poets and men of letters did not choose to forget this most outspoken enemy of railways; and the *John Ruskin*, built at Crewe works in 1914, did yeoman work for over 20 years as one of a team including names of such diverse association as *Charles Kingsley, Felicia Hemans, Lewis Carroll* and *Sir W. S. Gilbert*. It is to be doubted whether Ruskin, who disliked even the dainty steam gondola on Coniston Water, would have taken the act of the L.N.W.R. as a compliment!

Returning once more to creature comforts it is surprising to find that for nearly thirty years after the inception of passenger travel by rail little or no attempt was made to warm the carriage in cold weather. And yet another thirty years elapsed before we had progressed beyond the primitive foot-warmer—water-tight boxes of oblong shape filled with hot water. These were originally supplied only to first-class passengers, but even so became quite useless when the water cooled down. F. W. Webb, when Chief Mechanical Engineer of the London and North Western, applied his inventive genius to the problem of carriage heating, and from 1880 passengers enjoyed the use of a novel form of foot-warmer in which the heat was generated by the chemical action of soda acetate. The vessel containing this compound was heated in a vat of boiling water, prior to use, and the recrystallization of the salt as it cooled down gave off latent heat. It was the job of porters at intermediate stations to shake up these gadgets when they had cooled down so as to restore warmth; the process invariably provoked conversation between passengers, often breaking down the frigid silence of convention observed for hours between fellow travellers. It has even been suggested that Webb's foot-warmer was the prime cause of our modern figurative expression "to break the ice".

Even before the introduction of foot-warmers travel in the enclosed, though heatless, first-class carriages was luxury itself compared to the rigours of second- and third-class accommodation. The old open "boxes" provided for sixty standing passengers, and one reads of second-class passengers catching cold from the currents of air playing about their feet. The currents of air, it should be added, were due to holes in the floors specially provided to let out the rain! As a result of many complaints the Stockton and Darlington Railway was led to specifying for new rolling stock: "With these and all other coaches on the line, great care to be taken to make them airtight at the bottom." Steam heating was first introduced in 1884, but even with the modern systems there are occasions when the inherent difficulty of adjustment leaves no choice save between draughts from a partly opened window, and an insufferable "fug".

Until the recent introduction of the high-speed diesel Pullman trains air conditioning had so far been applied to only one day service in this country, the "Flying Scotsman"; but this apparent lag behind American practice is largely due to the pleasant summer conditions here, and to the comparative absence of cinder-throwing by our locomotives. On most lines in America one could not keep the windows open in summer for any length of time without everything inside the compartment becoming coated thickly with dust, both from the road and from the exhaust of the locomotive; and it is largely to provide for cool and pleasant travel in summer that air conditioning has been so widely adopted over there.

The discomfort of third-class travelling in early railway days was one factor leading to the "Regulation of Railways Act" of 1844. By this act all railways in the country were compelled to run at least one train a day, serving every station, and including enclosed carriages for third-class passengers, at a fare of one penny per mile. They became known as "Parliamentary" trains and for many years were renowned only for their slowness and the inconvenience of their timing. But gradually one penny per mile became the basic charge for railway travel, instead of a cheap rate confined to the slowest of passenger trains, though it was not until 1875, when the Midland Railway took the revolutionary step of abolishing second-class altogether, that third-class passengers began to get such luxuries as cushioned seats.

Hitherto the "seconds" had been cushioned and the "thirds" plain boards, and it was to a chorus of dire prophecies that the Midland scrapped nearly the whole of their third class carriages, and designated their existing "seconds" as "thirds". But instead of their receipts dwindling the increased comfort attracted business, and

167

rival companies were forced to improve the standard of their own third-class accommodation. Eventually one by one they too abolished the second-class until it survived only on the Continental boat express from London to Dover, Folkestone and Harwich, though the suburban services in North-east London retained them for many years. Recently however third class was re-designated "second". During the first World War the basic charge for travel was increased to $1\frac{3}{4}d$. per mile, though reduced to $1\frac{1}{2}d$. afterwards. Later, when competition with road transport increased, numerous cheap tickets were introduced, culminating in the monthly return, at "single fare and a third" for the double journey. The effect of this was virtually to bring back the basic charge to $1d$. a mile, for it was only on single tickets and returns extending over a period longer than a month that full fare was charged. Even through the great emergency of the second World War monthly return tickets remained available, though the charge was slightly increased to a little under $1\frac{1}{4}d$. per mile.

Mention of the suburban services of north-east London recalls the period, some 45 years ago, when the approaching end of steam traction was confidently predicted. The success of local electrification schemes abroad, and, of course, on the District and Metropolitan Railways in London, led in many quarters to the facile assumption that the British main line railways would soon be electrified. The advocates of electric traction promised that speeds of 30 m.p.h. would be obtained in 30 seconds from a dead start, a feat that was generally considered impossible with steam. To confound the theorists, James Holden, Locomotive Superintendent of the Great Eastern Railway, gave his design staff *carte blanche*, and under the leadership of Fred Russell, Chief Draughtsman at the Stratford Works, they produced an amazing locomotive, with ten coupled wheels. The Decapod, as she became known, exceeded expectations in achieving some remarkable feats of acceleration with heavy suburban trains, but she was too heavy for the existing track and the bridges.

The possibilities of steam had, however, been well and truly demonstrated, though it fell to Russell to devise in a totally different way the means for continuing the operation of the vast Great Eastern suburban service with steam traction. In 1915 he vacated the post of Chief Draughtsman to become Superintendent of Operations, and in this latter capacity he entirely reorganized the traffic working in and out of Liverpool Street Station, making it possible to bring in the business trains at the rate of 50 an hour, each of these conveying between 850 and 1,000 passengers! Every movement whether of loaded or empty trains, or of light engines, was planned out to the second; modifications were made to the track layout, and the success attending the general scheme of working may be gauged from the punctuality for which Liverpool Street became renowned.

For those who are so inclined timetables provide a fascinating study, while to those who are not they can be baffling in the extreme. It was in October 1839 that George Bradshaw issued the first timetable to show all trains then running in this country, and in December 1842 there appeared for the first time a regular monthly publication under the now familiar title of *Bradshaw's Railway Guide*. As the railway network of Great Britain grew so did "Bradshaw", and with the evident desire of the publishers for compactness, and the use of numerous cross-references the reading of it became a complicated business. In many parts of the country local publishers began to produce timetables of a regional character, and the Bristol firm of Evans and Arrowsmith, in introducing their guide in 1854, took a sly dig at "Bradshaw". "We have the greatest confidence in stating that our Time Tables (which are secured by copyright) will be found the most lucid, simple, and at the same time comprehensive, of any that have ever appeared. This desideratum, we feel assured, will be fully appreciated by the Public who must have met with almost insuperable difficulties in pondering over some of the cumbrous budgets which are monthly issued from the press."

By the year 1865 the complications of "Bradshaw" had become so notorious as to attract the attention of *Punch;* for eight consecutive weeks, in a droll series of articles, the asterisks, "daggers", footnotes, abbreviations, and what not were dilated upon, the outcome of which was of course to elevate "Bradshaw" to the level of a national institution. "Bradshaw" was much the same then as later, except in price. The original timetable of 1839 was sold at 1*s.*; the Guide of 1842 was 6*d.*, and thus the price remained till 1916 when war conditions caused an increase to 1*s.* In the enlightened days we are now living in the price has gone up and up until it finally reached twelve shillings. At this stage the proprietors found it uneconomic to continue, and Bradshaw ceased publication in May 1961.

In this sketch of the British Railways "then and now" I have touched upon locomotives and rolling stock, bridges and permanent way, signalling and brakes; but so far I have said nothing about the operating staff. In doing so now, to conclude the chapter I am turning to a corner of the country that has had but little attention in these pages, South Wales. It is here that the greatest contrast between past and present is to be found. The local railways, once independent but later mostly merged in the Great Western, worked their arduous ways up the mining valleys. Uphill their little tank engines toiled with loads of empty coal wagons, while downhill, often with fearfully inadequate brake power came the loaded trains for the docks at Newport and Cardiff. Sometimes as many as three locomotives were used simply to provide more brake power, but even then there were cases where heavily loaded trains came to grief. In 1878 there was a disastrous affair on the Brecon and Merthyr line, when a train of 36 wagons, with two engines at the front and one at the rear, got completely out of control on the very steep incline between Torpantau and Talybont. The gradient here is 1 in 38, and extends for nearly seven miles, and down this the runaway developed some very high speed. Near the foot of the incline the train left the road and was completely wrecked.

The men who operated the trains on such inclines under early railway conditions, when load limits were distinctly elastic must have possessed a rare mixture of nerve and skill. That they were subject to very strict discipline is evident from some of the rules to be found among Taff Vale regulations dated 1856. For instance Rule No. 40 reads:

"Not any instance of intoxication, singing, whistling or levity, while on duty, will be overlooked."

Then again

"Every person is to come on duty daily, clean in his person and clothes, shaved, and his boots blacked";

while another instruction has a quaint ring to-day:

"All persons, especially those in uniform, are to keep their hair cut."

Sabbatarianism was again in evidence, though strange enough with an eye to business; for Rule No. 26 read:

"It is urgently requested every person . . . on Sundays and Holy Days when he is not required on duty, that he will attend a place of worship, as it will be the means of promotion when vacancies occur."(!)

Perhaps the funniest of all related to the privileged few to whom free passes were granted.

"Persons having passes are to ride in the fourth wagon from the last in the train, and at all times in a sitting position upon the bottom of the wagon."

5

A Miscellany of Oddities, Anecdotes and Fiction

"Noodles", the charming and delightfully irresponsible heroine of some of Denis Mackail's gayest novels, usually managed to include at least one railway adventure among the succession of scrapes through which she flitted in every one of these tales; and as her world was that of the quietest English countryside, it was not the glamorous *Wagon-Lit* trains of the Continent, nor even our own crack expresses in which she travelled. The scene was laid on the country branch lines of Southern England, where the comedy of railway operation is played to the full.

In *Another Part of the Wood* the author deftly sets the stage thus:

"The local train followed its usual deliberate habits. Its engine left it and went for a little run by itself; came back presently with an empty horse-box, and hit the other coaches so as to show them what it had found; then stood still and panted as if it had just fetched somebody's stick out of the water, or occasionally sighed as if it were the most misunderstood engine on the whole of the line. Meanwhile the porters came back and played a game with some milk cans and large wooden boxes, pausing every now and then as though they weren't quite certain of the rules, and then beginning again with more noise than ever. . . ."

The journey was only a short one, but before its close a gentleman of very doubtful credentials had enlisted the sympathy of our tender-hearted heroine. The climax came with journey's end:

"As the train hiccupped over the points by the brickworks, half a mile this side of Pipping-fold, Noodles reached an inevitable decision and at the same moment thanked her stars that she had not reached it too late.

" '—not asking for charity,' the man was muttering hypnotically.

" 'No, No,' said Noodles, standing up and feeling for her dressing-bag on the rack. 'Of course not'.

"The man's eyes followed her greedily.

" 'But if everyone 'ad your kind 'eart, Miss'.

"The dressing-bag seemed to have become wedged into a tangle with the stringed instrument, the hockey stick and the umbrella; and as Noodles climbed on to the seat and tugged at it, the point of this last piece of property slipped through the meshes of the netting, making the deadlock even more complete than before.

" 'Bother!'

" 'Can I 'elp you, Missie?'

" 'No thank you, I can manage it if—There!'

"There! indeed. The brakes of that local train were always less remarkable for their delicacy than their power, and particularly was this the case on a sharp down-grade such as that which marks the approach to Pippingfold. Even so, however, Noodles would probably have recovered herself if she hadn't been standing on the seat, and if the hockey stick hadn't chosen that precise moment to come loose from the general jumble—which it certainly wouldn't have done if she hadn't been pulling it quite so hard. And even then it wouldn't have caught the unfortunate stranger such a frightful whack on the side of the head, if in his eagerness to snatch at Noodles' purse as soon as it appeared—for there is really no other explanation for his behaviour both before and after this accident—he hadn't been standing on tiptoe just behind her.

"So at the word 'There!' all these things happened in far less time than it takes to describe; and the man gave a squeal of surprise and agony, and Noodles gave a squeal of surprise and remorse; and the stout little station master came trotting up, and opened the door, and began shouting very excitedly; and the porter and the man who drives the hired Ford came trundling to his assistance, also shouting; and the station master said 'Well done, Miss, we've got him this time'; and the man in gaiters opened the other door and jumped out on to the line, and

175

ran away, and disappeared—though not before
the engine-driver had tried to hit him with a piece
of coal at a distance of about seventy-five yards,
and had failed in this gallant attempt."

A delicious sample of railway fiction, yet one that
in its placid background breathes out the true spirit of
the old Kent and East Sussex line, and many another
somnolent branch.

Richard Wyndham writes of the Kent and East Sussex,
in *South Eastern Survey:* "The track, as green and
beautiful as a chickweedy disused canal, finds its way
through hedges of willows which rap and brush the carriage sides, or across Bodiam marshes where herons
stand by the line—no longer perturbed. There are few
roads through this stretch of country, which remains
much the same as when the peasants first complained
about the iron monster which had desecrated their
land. . . .

"Northiam appeared to be an important station: I
was joined by a passenger with a perambulator; and
some endless shunting was done. The guard-pointsman
could give no fixed time of departure, but he would hold
the train for me, of course, if I wished to walk up the
village for a glass of beer. . . ."

A very curious old line, which survived in all its primitive details of working until 1935, was to be found in
the hill-country of south Shropshire. It was part of a
scheme promoted in 1859 to provide a cross-country link
between the Shrewsbury and Hereford Railway on the
one hand, and what afterwards became the main line of

176

the Cambrian system. It was planned to run from a junction near Craven Arms north-westwards to Montgomery, while from Lydham Heath, a station about half way between the two trunk lines, a short branch was proposed to Bishop's Castle, with the junction points arranged for direct running between Bishop's Castle and Montgomery. From the very outset the company was in serious financial difficulties, and the section of line between Lydham Heath and Montgomery was never constructed at all; so that throughout the seventy years of its parlous existence all trains on the shuttle service between Craven Arms and Bishop's Castle had to reverse direction at Lydham Heath, a comic state of affairs in a journey of but 10 miles. To the bitter end, in 1935, they had no telegraph, or telephone, and although the line was single no token was needed as the company kept only one engine in steam at a time. When the grouping of the railways took place in 1923 the Bishop's Castle was left high and dry, an independent concern, and with the development of convenient road motor services in the district any usefulness it might have had soon vanished. In the end the staff had shrunk to one driver, one fireman, two booking clerks, and two station mistresses.

Another picturesque little railway which fell a victim to road competition was the narrow-gauge line between Lynton and Barnstaple. This was sponsored in 1895 by certain influential gentlemen of Lynton; they themselves were however without any practical experience in railway construction and working, and the professional advice they took was not of the best. In putting forward the scheme the advantages of the proposed narrow gauge of 1 ft. 11½ ins. were stressed, as permitting the use of sharp curves and so reducing earthworks to a minimum in the very hilly Devon countryside; but the Engineer apparently went ahead on the facile assumption that nothing more than ordinary soil would have to be dug from the shallow cuttings. To the chagrin of all concerned most of the cuttings had to be blasted from solid rock, and the total cost of construction was double that included in the estimates. It proved a well-nigh crippling start to this ambitious local venture, but the novelty of the small trains and the charm of the scenery made the railway very popular with holiday makers.

Quaint little tank engines, with tall chimneys, cowcatchers and highly-polished steam domes went chugging up the 1 in 50 gradients towards Lynton, over the breezy hinterland of the North Devon coast; the streams, and the woodlands, the constantly winding track, the red-brown soil, the distant views of Exmoor—all combined to give the Lynton and Barnstaple Railway a delightful character of its own. Shortly after the grouping of the main line companies it was purchased by the Southern Railway. But even in its earliest days difficulty was found in competing with horse brakes, and primitive motor cars, and in the post-grouping era, Southern Railway management notwithstanding, there was little hope of the line paying its way. To the end however it remained very popular with summer visitors, but the season was relatively short, and local patronage of the line almost vanished. And so at the end of the summer season of 1935 the Southern Railway closed it.

Some thirty years ago, my mother was travelling from Euston to Barrow-in-Furness for the first time, and was lucky enough to have as travelling companion a Lancashire man, who really knew the North. A talkative fellow-traveller all too frequently degenerates into a frightful bore ere one's destination is reached, but it was far otherwise on my mother's first trip to Barrow. Besides talking vividly of the countryside he knew and loved, her companion had the gift of a rich sense of humour. And when the train turned aside at Carnforth from the princely London and North Western, and began to follow the sinuous track of the Furness Railway, along the coast and across the wide sandy estuaries of the Lakeland rivers, the railway itself, and its reputed vagaries came within the orbit of conversation.

Some of these yarns, though surrounded by a wealth of local colour, were strongly reminiscent of similar anecdotes told against the South Eastern, the London Chatham and Dover, and other nineteenth century sluggards—primrose picking by engine crews and such like. But then came the final shot: the train had breasted the heavy ascent from Ulverston, and was crossing Lindal Moor; alongside the main tracks were a group of sidings crowded with wagons dusty red from carrying iron ore. The raconteur chose his moment with precision. "There," he pointed, "is where an engine disappeared down a hole." The gust of laughter was cut short by his announcement that journey's end was now at hand, and further details were neither sought nor given. But of all the improbable happenings related on the Furness section of the journey that last was probably the only one

179

to have any foundation in fact. More than that—it was literally true!

What actually happened was this:

The district around Lindal Moor is honeycombed with iron ore workings and on September 22nd 1892, a subsidence occurred beneath the main line. One of the standard goods engines, a powerful type for that period—was shunting at the time; under its weight the road gave way, and the engine settled down head first into the chasm which had so suddenly appeared. The driver and fireman managed to jump clear, and with the ground at first sinking only gradually the tender was saved. The breakdown gang, having achieved this considerable success, went back to Barrow to bring their heaviest tackle for lifting the engine; but on their return they found to their astonishment that it had entirely disappeared!

Although belonging wholly to the Lake District, the Furness Railway was very much a coastal route, following for most of its length what George Stephenson considered the only practicable way from North Lancashire to the Scottish Border. A few short branches struck up valleys towards the central mountain massif, and to travel up these lines was exhilarating not only for the splendour of the passing scene but also in the smartness of the working. But there was another Lakeland railway that more than made up for the efficiency of the Furness branch lines; this was the Ravenglass and Eskdale. Most readers will have made the acquaintance of this line in its present form as a fascinating miniature railway, with jolly little open carriages, and some equally jolly small-scale locomotives.

But there was a time when the gauge was wider, the passenger vehicles were closed in, and some attempt was made to imitate ordinary railway working. "Imitate" is scarcely the correct word, for surely no more ramshackle concern ever had the face to call itself a railway. It was originally built as a "light railway", of 2 ft. 9 in. gauge for conveying iron ore from a group of mines near the foot of Scafell to the coast. Passenger traffic came later, but after a brief spell of prosperity this little railway fell upon evil times; somehow a service of trains was kept going but with the original equipment and little or nothing in the way of track maintenance. "Austerity" was not the word for the dilapidated box-like carriages in use up to 1908, while their drunken reeling along that winding track had to be experienced to be fully appreciated. For some time the railway was in Chancery.

The 15-inch gauge line of today is very smartly run, but for some time after the conversion the locomotive working was erratic and sometimes highly amusing. There were some quaint old tank engines, purchased from the Duke of Westminster's private railway at Eaton Hall, of a kind that might be termed "contractor's" locomotives; they trundled along like old cart horses, and were in extraordinary contrast to the beautiful scale-model express engines *Sanspareil* and *Colossus*, built by Bassett-Lowke's. These little flyers used to dash away at a speed that was somewhat disconcerting on the roughly laid track of that time. The grades were, however, exceedingly steep in places, and with heavy holiday trains the pace would get slower and slower till chivalrous male passengers jumped out, and gave some invaluable human banking assistance. But once over the crest of the particular incline away would go the heedless *Colossus* or *Sanspareil* in a tremendous downhill acceleration, leaving the astonished benefactors to sprint alongside and jump on board as best they could!

To experience the supreme thrill of narrow gauge railroading one must however ride on the miniature locomotives themselves. On the Eskdale railway the Bassett-Lowke engines were built more or less correctly to scale with the gauge, and were thereby limited in power. When the Romney, Hythe and Dymchurch line was constructed the locomotives were built to altogether larger proportions, though still retaining the 15-inch gauge. If a Romney express engine was enlarged to the length and height of a London and North Eastern Pacific the gauge of the full-scale engine would be 3 ft. 6 in. instead of the standard 4 ft. 8½ in. This adjustment of the proportions does not in any way spoil the scale-model appearance of the locomotives, and it enables them to be made much more powerful; furthermore the increased width makes it possible for two persons to ride in the cab. While the Eskdale has the charm of a mountain setting, with a track working its way along the flanks of heather-clad fells, the Romney has a straight, level road where you really can "run". It was to test the capacity of these remarkable little engines that I was privileged, a few years before the war, to ride in the cab. Quite apart from the technical side of the business I was astonished to find how very much like the real thing it was: the bumping, the hard riding, all the familiar footplate smells were present; but strangest of all was the extraordinary illu-

182

sion of high speed, when travelling at 25 to 30 m.p.h. I suppose it was created through sitting so very close to the ground.

For part of the run out to Dungeness I drove the engine and while I was thus engrossed a curious incident occurred. We were racing along the shingle between Littlestone and Dungeness when we sighted a white object on the line ahead. The driver, a retired Southern Railway man, soon spotted it was a sheet of newspaper and suggested easing up, telling me that a train had once been derailed through a similar piece becoming caught in the wheels. We slowed up to about 5 m.p.h., but sure enough this piece caught up too, and we duly stopped in order to disentangle it from under the engine! Writing of accidents, a curious inversion of the usual order of things took place at a level crossing on this line a few years ago. Through some contretemps a motor lorry collided with a train; but although the miniature locomotive was overturned and several of the coaches were derailed, the only casualty, and a slight one at that, was the lorry driver.

The subject of railway accidents in general is a very interesting one. In many a smash there is a host of different contributory causes, and upon constant and scientific analysis of these, in each and every case, have been built up many of the principles on which the safe operation of the railways of today depend. In this respect the travelling public is indebted, to a degree far greater than is generally realised, to the work of the inspecting officers, first of the Board of Trade, and since 1920 of the Ministry of Transport. This duty has always been carried out by officers of the Royal Engineers, and among others, the names of Colonel Yolland, Major-General Hutchinson, Colonel von Donop and Colonel Sir John Pringle should be associated equally with railway engineers and administrators in the building up of the railway system and service as it is today. It is perhaps significant of the esteem in which the Ministry of Transport Inspectorate is held that when a disaster on the East Indian Railway suggested a serious defect in the design of the locomotive, the Government of India invited the then Chief Inspecting Officer, Colonel Sir Alan Mount, to preside over a committee of inquiry.

The contributory cause of accidents can be broadly classified under three headings: failures of material, or faults in workmanship, as when a fractured tie-bar brought down a large portion of the roof of Charing Cross Station; faulty principles of operation, as with one early form of continuous brake, and failures of the human element—acts of simple forgetfulness, misreading signals and such like. But again there is a small number of accidents, the primary cause of which has never been explained. Colonel Von Donop had a very difficult task in conducting the enquiry into the Grantham accident of 1906, in which one of the night expresses from King's Cross to the North was involved.

The train had stopped at Peterborough, and had, as usual, changed engines there. Grantham was the next stop, and when the train approached, the signals at the north end of that station were at danger. It just happened that the points beyond the station were set for the Nottingham branch; but there was nothing irregular in their being so, as they lay beyond the signals that were at danger. But instead of stopping in Grantham Station the Scottish express ran through at full speed, passed the north signals, and took the sharp curve on to the branch at a speed estimated at more than 60 m.p.h. Somewhat naturally the engine left the road; many of the coaches were wrecked, and there was heavy loss of life.

The Inspecting Officer had the difficult task of trying to discover why the train ran away. The driver was a reliable and fully experienced man, who had worked the train on the previous night. He and his fireman were killed in the crash so that the Inspector could only base his conclusions upon inferences drawn from the statements of witnesses, and from examination of the locomotive itself afterwards. The evidence was, however, wholly inconclusive, and the reason for this unfortunate occurrence remained a complete mystery. A theory was advanced that the driver might suddenly have been taken ill; that the fireman in his consternation went immediately to his mate's assistance, not realising how close they were to Grantham, and while he was thus engaged they ran through the station. Whatever the cause the locomotive—No. 276, one of the celebrated Ivatt "Atlantics"—was regarded as an engine of ill-omen for many years on the Great Northern Railway.

Exactly 25 years afterwards a colleague was travelling by the "Queen of Scots" Pullman express from Leeds to London, and noticed that the running was not quite up to standard. On arrival at King's Cross he found that the engine was No. 276, or to be strictly correct 3276, for such she was renumbered by the L.N.E.R. My friend spoke to the driver, who remarked: "Oh, she's not a good engine; never has been since that night." He paused and then: "You know, Sir, it was just 25 years yesterday since the smash, and going down to Leeds yesterday I couldn't help wondering to myself whether she might go and take the wrong road at Grantham on the way down." Here in a railwayman was the same kind of superstition that sailors show towards an unlucky ship.

Some years later I had occasion to ride on the engine working the 9.35 a.m. express from Sheffield to Leicester. Prior to this under a motive-power re-allocation scheme a number of Great Northern "Atlantic" engines had been transferred to the Great Central Section, and going through the lists at the time I had been amused to note that the Great Northern people had taken care to include 3276 in this batch! The incident had passed from my mind until I came on to the platform at Sheffield that morning and saw 3276, bright and clean as a new pin, standing on the centre road and waiting to take the 9.35 a.m. express. The cheery Yorkshiremen in charge of her evidently knew nothing of her past history, and were full of praise for the class as a whole, and when we got away it was to make a brilliant run to Leicester. So much for the engine of ill omen!

Accidents due to failure of apparatus can usually, through scientific analysis, be fully explained. So also can those unhappy occasions when an act of simple forgetfulness on the part of a signalman or driver leads to disaster. The worst accident in British railway history was caused by a signalman's error. It occurred on the Saturday before Whitsun 1915, and at that early stage in the first World War it was still a case of "holidays as usual". On account of heavy traffic, the midnight express from Euston to Glasgow had been delayed on the English part of the journey, so much so that a Caledonian local had been despatched from Carlisle ahead of the express, instead of following it in the usual way. This local was run out as far as Quintinshill, a signal box some two miles north of Gretna, and there backed on to the up road to clear the down road for the express.

The signalmen were changing shift at the time, and shortly after the arrival of the local the box at Kirkpatrick, 2¾ miles to the north, offered a troop train. Incredible though it may seem this train was accepted and the signals lowered for it to pass, when all the time the local train was standing on the very track it would use—what is more, just outside the box; in fact the signalman concerned had only a few minutes previously travelled from Gretna to his work by this very train! On a down gradient and running under clear signals, the troop train approached at over 70 m.p.h., and although after sighting the obstruction the driver had time to shut off steam and get the brakes on the speed was estimated at fully 60 m.p.h. when his locomotive ran head-on into the local train.

In this terrific crash, wreckage of both trains was flung in all directions, but there was scarcely time to do anything before the midnight express from Euston approached. Travelling fast, and drawn by two engines, it ploughed through the debris of the first collision, adding to the already-grievous loss of life and wholesale destruction of railway stock. Fire broke out among the shattered wooden carriages of the troop train, and many who were trapped perished before they could be extricated; in all 227 persons were killed, and 250 injured— a terrible consequence of one man's negligence.

In early days those responsible for repair and maintenance of the track used the timetable only to guide them when planning operations that involved complete occupation of the line. Today it seems to us a hazardous proceeding, but trains were then not so frequent, and in the prevailing conditions the arrangement generally worked well enough. Inevitably, though, there were instances in which disregard of the safety regulations caused accidents. An especially flagrant case occurred on the South Eastern Railway in 1865, near Staplehurst, on that magnificent racing stretch through the Weald between Ashford and Tonbridge.

On June 9th in that year it was decided to renew the last of the timber baulks in a bridge over a small river called the Beult. The only train likely to affect the arrangements was the boat express from Folkestone, which, since the packet-boats could at that time only berth at high tide, varied in its time from day to day. The foreman in charge of the work on the bridge consulted his timetable and noted that the train was due to pass Headcorn two miles east of the bridge at 5.20 p.m. Unfortunately he was careless enough to look at the wrong page in the book. The time he noted was that for the following day, the actual scheduled time was 3.11 p.m. Worse still, he failed to carry out a most important regulation: that a flagman should proceed 1,000 yards from any obstruction, putting down a detonator every

250 yards, and two at his point of duty. At Staplehurst the flagman only went 550 yards, and put down no detonators at all. The signals, like those at Abbots Ripton were normally in the clear position so that the foreman platelayer would not know when the train was coming.

The tidal boat-train passed Headcorn exactly on time, running at about 50 m.p.h. The first warning the driver received of any obstruction was the red flag of the man stationed 550 yards before the bridge, and with the brake then in use this was, of course, quite inadequate. The train came upon the bridge at between 20 and 30 m.p.h. to find a gap of 42 feet, where one line of rails had been removed. The engine crashed down on the longitudinal timber baulks, remaining upright somehow, and by its own momentum reached the other side of the gap, dragging after it the first three vehicles of the train; but the couplings broke between the third and fourth vehicle, and the rest of the train having no continuous brakes piled up behind, swerved to the left, and crashed over into the swampy field below. Some of the coaches that might have stayed on the bridge were pulled over and landed upside down in the stream. Charles Dickens happened to be a passenger and there is a particularly vivid account from his pen in a letter written to a friend four days afterwards:

"I was in the only carriage that did not go over into the stream. It was caught upon the turn by some of the ruins of the bridge and hung suspended and balanced in an impossible manner.

189

Two ladies were my fellow passengers . . . suddenly we were off the rail and beating the ground as the car of a half-emptied balloon might. . . . We were then all tilted down together in a corner of the carriage (which was locked) and stopped. . . . I got out through the window without the the least notion of what had happened . . . with great caution and stood upon the step . . . looking down I saw the bridge gone and nothing below me but the line of rail . . . there was an open swampy field fifteen feet below them and nothing else . . . I saw all the rest of the train except the two baggage vans, down in the stream, . . . No imagination can conceive the ruin of the carriages."

Dickens, although suffering from a lameness in one leg, worked for some hours among the injured and dying, and what he himself called "the terrific nature of the scene", coupled no doubt with the violent shaking up he received when his own carriage went off the road, seriously affected his health for the rest of his life. It is singular that his death occurred on the fifth anniversary of the accident.

During the Victorian era the comparative novelty of railways as a mode of travel and the wonderment of the public at the increasing power and complexity of locomotives no doubt encouraged dramatists and other writers to introduce railway incidents into their works. With some their sense of the dramatic overrode all technical considerations, and the scene which the author of an old-style melodrama intended to be a really blood-curdling climax was often made farcical by the crudely amateurish representation of the train, signal-box or other railway piece. This was the kind of play in which the climax takes place on a railway line, with the heroine chained to the metals, an express train approaching, while the villain (in evening-dress of course), and the hero fight it out in the four-foot!

More recently Arnold Ridley has given us "The Ghost Train" and "The Wrecker", in both of which plays the railway setting is accurately portrayed, so far as technicalities are concerned. But unlike those of America the British railways have in actual fact never been the scene of dramatic hold-ups, or sensational acts arising from some terrific human drama. Attempts have been made, as in the film "The Flying Scotsman", to stage such stories against a British railway background, but the idea of a devastating blonde making her perilous way along the footboards of an express in motion, and then clambering over the tender amid the coal, to arrive on the footplate in the nick of time to save her fiancé, the fireman, from a horrible death, strikes one as altogether fantastic. Mention of the movies reminds me that in the film version of "The Ghost Train", the train, between its last stealthy departure from the quay and the plunge to doom through the open swing bridge some fifteen minutes later, changed engines twice!

The writings of the Victorian novelists often give an insight into travelling conditions of sixty to seventy years ago. With Dickens the human side of travel is of course uppermost though his railway observations are quite accurate. They were used in a recent issue of *The Dickensian* by T. W. Hill, in the course of an analysis trying to establish the period of the story *The Mystery of Edwin Drood*. "Cloisterham", of the story, can more or less readily be identified as Rochester, and from this starting point, in tracing the comings and goings of the various characters it is clear that Dickens had an intimate knowledge of railway routes and facilities, not only at the time the tale was written, but also at a considerably earlier period.

A minor mystery, however, is why the people in the story used the railway at all to travel to London. They could have gone by direct road-coach from Rochester, a distance of only 29 miles. Instead Dickens took them 21 miles by road to Maidstone Road Station (now Paddock Wood on the South Eastern main line to Dover), whence it was then a 46-mile journey to London Bridge. The present short route via Sevenoaks was not built until some twenty years after the supposed date of the story, and the journey would have had to be made via Redhill. One is led to the conclusion that Dickens felt he must include some railway travelling, and having settled upon Rochester for the scene of the tale he took his characters to what was the nearest railway station at the time he had in mind. It was not until 1849 that the North Kent line reached Strood, whereas the travelling facilities alluded to by Dickens would date the story as between 1842 and 1844.

The adventures of Sherlock Holmes often took him and Dr. Watson by train, but except for one notable occasion when the great detective passed an idle moment

38 Power Control Room Crewe, for electric traction supply, London
Midland main line electrifications

39 Divisional Traffic Control Office, Crewe, London Midland Region

40 Crack Express of the 1920s: "The Lancastrian" of the L.M.S., Manchester to Euston, taking water at 75 m.p.h. at Castlethorpe, Bucks. The engine is an ex-L.N.W.R. "Claughton" class 4-6-0

41 Motive Power of the 1960s: the prototype "Deltic" diesel-electric locomotive (3300 h.p.) on a trial run near Preston, Lancs.

42 The culmination of a great tradition: Patrick Stirling's final express passenger design for the Great Northern Railway; the latest and largest variety of the eight-foot bogie singles, built in 1894. Stirling's engines, throughout the 30 years he was at Doncaster, all had domeless "straight-back" boilers

DONCASTER STEAM, GREAT AND SMALL

43 The most powerful express type ever built at Doncaster: Sir Nigel Gresley's giant 2–8–2 "Cock o' the North", built in 1934. This engine and the other five of the "P2" class were designed for working on the difficult route between Edinburgh and Aberdeen, across the Forth and Tay Bridges

44 The "Midland Pullman": high speed diesel express running between London and Manchester, here shown passing Silkstream Junction, near Hendon, Middlesex

TRAINS OF THE NEW AGE

45 Freight train on the London Midland Region near Watford, Herts. The engine is a British Standard 2–10–0 of Class 9F. The very last steam locomotive to be built for British Railways was of this design, and it is named "Evening Star". Although primarily designed for freight these locomotives are extraordinarily versatile, and have been recorded up to 90 m.p.h. on express trains

46 British trains of the future: one of the new high speed 3000 h.p. electric locomotives of the London Midland Region, in the modernised Manchester terminus, formerly known as London Road, and now renamed Piccadilly.

47 A Modern Signal Control Room: the operating panel and illuminated diagram at Newcastle-on-Tyne, North Eastern Region

48 A vast array of semaphore signals at Newcastle Central, 1906

STATION APPROACHES OLD AND NEW

49 The approach to Manchester Piccadilly, 1962, showing the new signal
box, and the overhead equipment for electric traction.

by a lightning estimation of the speed of the West of England express in which he and the Doctor were travelling, there is little of direct railway background in their journeyings. It is in that magnificent yarn *The Adventure of the Bruce Partington Plans* that Conan Doyle reveals his intimate knowledge of railway working. In following out Holmes's swift unravelling of the mystery, in tracing the connexion between the disappearance of the secret plans of a new submarine and the finding of a young man's body on the Inner Circle line near Aldgate, those with an expert knowledge would also detect that certain liberties had been taken with the railway geography of Gloucester Road. But save for the most pedantic these are of no account, and the railway details are as convincing as the rest of Holmes's masterly analysis of the problem.

An Inner Circle train was concerned, and at that time of course it would have been steam hauled, by one of those supremely ugly, yet most efficient Beyer-Peacock tank engines. Had the train chanced instead to be one on the Outer Circle service, the body, far from remaining on the roof all the way from Gloucester Road till the sharp curve at Minories Junction, might have rolled off at the very first start with one particular engine. The "Outer Circle" was really not a circle at all, but merely a horsehoe as it consisted of a shuttle service between Broad Street and Mansion House, by way of Hampstead Heath, Willesden and Earl's Court. It was operated by the London and North Western Railway, utilizing running powers over the Underground line from Earl's Court to the Mansion House.

The engines working on this service were mostly of the same general type as used on the Underground trains proper, but then one day a stranger was introduced. In the fourth chapter of this book I referred to the Webb compound express engines on the L.N.W.R. and their antics in starting, or not starting. Another noticeable characteristic, when they did eventually get away, was a pronounced fore and aft surging motion, felt throughout the train. Webb in his enthusiasm also applied the compound system to a few local tank engines, and one of these, No. 687, was put on to the Outer Circle. The result is best described in the words of the late E. L. Ahrons, a great locomotive historian, and a great wit too: "Had the London & North Western tank engines had names like the tender engines," he wrote, "I would have respectfully suggested the name *Fore and Aft* for 687. . . . I had some experience of it myself—on one occasion when leaving Victoria (Underground) a carriage full of passengers were swinging backwards and forwards after the manner of a University 'eight'."

It is surprising to what extent the railway of today provide a link with the customs and occupations of olden times in various parts of the country. At Euston, in normal times at any rate, may be witnessed an act that perpetuates a custom continued practically unbroken for centuries. It is 8.30 p.m., and the Holyhead "sleeper" is drawn up. Far away up No. 13 platform, beyond the glitter and animation of the passenger coaches, beyond even the serenity of the sleeping cars, a burly postman comes from somewhere in the dusk; in his hand he swings a leather pouch rather like that used for single line tablet working. Out of curiosity the onlooker walks up to the van door, and the pouch is seen to contain a watch, for which the postmaster of the T.P.O. is signing a receipt. Thus, every night of the year, is carried on a tradition dating back to the time when the Irish mail was conveyed by coach to Holyhead, and even earlier than that, to the days of the galloping post boys. Every day the King's Time was sent out from London to the Irish Capital, though since 1940 the running of the Irish mail has been suspended.

Signal box names often give clues to a piece of interesting local history. Doncaster is nowadays associated with the building of locomotives, making butter-scotch, coal mining, and not least, the St. Leger. But the name of the town alone belies any suggestion that it is a modern settlement, and some of the signal box names locate approximately features of the town and district that have now disappeared. The old marsh gate, for example, where the north road passed through the town walls and struck out for the low lying country north of the River Don, is recalled by the modern Marshgate Junction, where the Scottish and West Riding main lines converge. Nearby is Frenchgate Junction, close to the site of a Franciscan Friary. Frenchgate itself is the name of a street, and it seems probable that this name owes its origin to the Friary. In the town records it is spelt Frenschgaite in 1529, and Frankyschgate in 1361. Travellers approaching Doncaster from the south may have noticed a signal box with the seemingly inappropriate name of Decoy. It stands at a point where there are sidings in every direction as far as the eye can see, and were one to try and count them the coal trucks would surely run into several thousands. But these extensive yards stand on ground that was once a vast game decoy, used to provide sport for the local gentry.

There are many other quaint and unusual signal box names, such as "Bo-Peep Junction", St. Leonards, taking its title from a neighbouring tavern. At York the former North Eastern Railway in conformity with its usual practice gave each one of the many signal boxes in the station approaches an individual name, so that one found Chaloners Whin Junction, Dringhouses, Water-works, and then to add a truly classical touch, Severus. The London and North Western, once so picturesque in its engine names, was wholly utilitarian so far as signal boxes were concerned, and at the bigger centres one noted a whole series of numbered boxes, "Euston No. 4", "Carlisle No. 13" and so on. It would seem that under L.N.E.R. management the old North Eastern was falling under the same spell, for once-splendid "Severus" has recently been changed to "York Yard North".

There is no denying that in the naming of locomotives most of the charm and spontaneity that characterized early railway days has now been lost. For this the systematized class naming introduced on the Great Western some forty years ago has been largely respon-sible. Like many another unfortunate modern trait it had small beginnings. To take one particular example, successive batches of a class of sixty express engines were given master names: the first ten were "Stars"—*Dog Star*, *Evening Star*, *Shooting Star*, and so on; the "Knights" came next, followed by "Kings", "Queens",

196

"Princes" and "Princesses". In each batch there were just enough titles to keep to the general plan, and provide names that were good and suitable *as names*.

The trouble began when the practice was extended to lesser lights in the locomotive stud. Having introduced, shortly after the first World War, a short series of "Abbeys", and a longer one of "Castles", including many beautiful and interesting names, someone in authority decided that a new class of mixed traffic engines should be named after "Halls". It was not enough that the first batch should bear the titles of country houses which to the average person were quite unknown; the process was continued till it became necessary, in a desperate search for more names, to include such appellations as *Albert Hall, Bingley Hall* and *Queen's Hall*. So matters went on until over two hundred engines had been so named. The same painful procedure, fortunately not so long drawn out, was followed with other mixed traffic classes which were named after "Manors" and "Granges".

The Great Western never had a finer nor a more diverse series of names than those given to the stately "single wheelers" built for the narrow gauge express services just about the time of the final conversion from broad to narrow gauge. There was no particular plan in naming these ornate, beautiful engines; some had the names of old broad gauge celebrities, others were named after members of the Royal Family, and lastly, perhaps most appealing of all, were those carrying names that were household words in the West Country. Thus taking a few at random, one found *Courier, Iron Duke, Racer* and *Swallow*, among the revivals of old broad gauge names; *Empress of India, Duchess of Teck* and *Duke of Connaught* were typical of the dignified Royal names, and then one came across *Flying Dutchman, White Horse, Westward Ho!, Sir Francis Drake* and *Lorna Doone*—lovely satisfying names that breathed the very spirit of the West.

The practice of handing down names from one generation of locomotives to the next enjoyed a long spell of popularity on the London and North Western Railway. Many of the names borne by engines running in 1922, when the L.N.W.R. became part of the one time L.M.S system can be traced back to the days of the Grand Junction Railway. The first ten locomotives built at Crewe works provide a striking example; no less than seven of those ten names were carried by express passenger engines in service in 1918—*Prince Albert, Apollo, Albion, Mersey, Belted Will, Saddleback* and *Princess*. Incidentally these seven names of 1845 are together representative of the policy followed by the L.N.W.R. throughout its history, wherein mythology, legend and personalities of the day were gloriously mixed with place names, symbols of patriotism, and purely expressive appellations like *Thunderer, Spitfire* and *Hurricane*.

In applying these names there was something of that magical touch that inspires the selection of names for destroyers in the Royal Navy. Here are seven taken in succession from the L.N.W.R. 1912 list *Gibraltar, Giraffe, Gladiator, Gladstone, Glatton, Glendower, Glowworm*. Two further examples show something of

198

the originality of certain titles chosen. There was the little "Whitworth" class express engine No. 2158 named *Sister Dora*, in memory of a Walsall nurse. Miss Dorothy Pattison, whose untiring efforts and devotion to duty in a terrible epidemic of small-pox eventually led to her own death. It would have been a sufficient honour to the lady had the engine been named *Dorothy Pattison*, but it so happened that the regular turn of duty for this locomotive took it daily through Walsall. Thus it was indeed a happy inspiration that gave it instead the name that was on everyone's lips when "Sister Dora" wrote so shining a page in the history of that town.

A gesture of altogether wider significance was made by the London and North Western Railway in 1919 when a new engine of the well-known "Sir Gilbert Claughton" class was named *Patriot*, in memory of the company's men who gave their lives in the war of 1914–18. This engine was specially numbered 1914. The lead of the L.N.W.R. in this respect was followed by two other British railways, the Great Central, which named an engine *Valour*, and the London Brighton and South Coast, with one named *Remembrance*. The idea even spread to India, where the Great Indian Peninsular Railway named one of their express engines *Hero*.

There can surely have been no stranger engine name than that carried by No. 90 of that same "Whitworth" class, *Luck of Edenhall*. This refers to an heirloom of the Great Cumbrian family of Musgrave, whose seat is at Eden Hall near Penrith. It is a beautiful goblet, and legend couples the family fortunes with those of the gob-

199

let itself. So runs Longfellow's version of a ballad by Uhland:

> "This glass of flashing crystal tall,
> Gave to my Sires the Fountain-Sprite;
> She wrote in it 'If this glass doth fall,
> Farewell then O Luck of Edenhall'."

A picturesque legend indeed, but what railway save the North Western would have named a locomotive after it!

The Scottish partner of the L.N.W.R., the Caledonian, did not make a regular practice of naming its locomotives. There were, however, a few isolated cases and amongst these two became very famous. The first was the *Dunalastair*, a grand, sonorous Scots name in itself; but it came to have a far greater significance than that of a Highland estate on Loch Rannoch, albeit that of Mr. J. C. Bunten, then Chairman of the Caledonian Railway. The locomotive *Dunalastair*, built in 1896, was the first of a series of highly successful designs which put the Caledonian in the forefront of British railway speed. The designer was that fine engineer and great personality, John F. McIntosh, whose locomotives were characterized by their simplicity and beauty of outline, and for their seemingly unlimited steaming powers.

McIntosh had an amazing career. At the age of 14 he joined the Scottish North Eastern Railway, becoming a fireman five years later, and afterwards a driver. As a result of a personal accident on the railway he lost his right arm, but he overcame this disability, and with one promotion after another he rose to the position of Chief Inspector of the Running Department on the Caledonian

Railway in 1891, 31 years after he had joined the service. Finally, in 1895, he became Chief Locomotive, Carriage, and Wagon Superintendent, and no chief can ever have been held in greater esteem and affection by his staff.

The second Caledonian engine, another McIntosh product, was that now almost legendary giant, No. 903 *Cardean*, which in 1906 and for nearly ten years afterwards worked "The Corridor" express, the 2 p.m. from Glasgow to Carlisle, and returned on the corresponding northbound train at 8.13 p.m.; and for quite half of her lengthy innings on that veritable queen of Anglo-Scottish expresses she was driven by one man, David Gibson, of Polmadie shed, Glasgow. *Cardean* was named after the estate of another Caledonian director, Mr. Edward Cox; it is situated near Alyth, in Perthshire. After a time the engine became as great an institution as the Corridor train itself; and working on the same turn year in, year out, with the same engine Gibson grew to know his work with an intimacy scarcely to be comprehended nowadays. As a result his running was like clock-work. This association of one driver, one engine, and one train for so long a period was probably unique. On *Cardean* was to be seen an example of the "private" embellishments with which certain Caledonian drivers adorned their engines. The regulator handle of *Cardean* was distinguished by a beautiful piece of brass filigree work, in which were embedded two burnished halfpennies.

The one-time rivalry between the Caledonian and the Glasgow and South Western was not merely a healthy competition between two extremely enterprising concerns; it was a deadly enmity, pursued with the utmost vigour by even the humblest members of the rank and file of both companies. Nowhere was this rivalry more openly manifested than on the combined rail and steamer services from Glasgow to the Clyde Coast resorts of Dunoon and Rothesay. There was a late afternoon express from Glasgow serving both places. Rival trains left the respective Glasgow termini within a few minutes of each other, and raced to Greenock. The "Sou' West" had the shorter rail distance, $25\frac{1}{2}$ miles from St. Enoch to Princes Pier, while the Caledonian timed the arrival of their train at Gourock—at the western end of the bay—so that their steamer would just be casting off as the G. & S.W.R. boat drew abreast. Then would follow an absolutely neck and neck race across the firth to Dunoon, where the piermaster had the delicate task of deciding who should take precedence.

In the heat of competition the timings of the boat trains were cut minute by minute until the Caledonian were running the $26\frac{1}{4}$ miles from Glasgow Central to Gourock in 32 minutes. Considering the nature of the road, the need for slow running out of Glasgow, the congested line to Paisley, and the severe speed restriction enforced there, this average of nearly 50 m.p.h. was amazing. To make sure of things the Caledonian used the "Dunalastair" engines. But the pace was too hot to be comfortable, and before long a deputation of season-ticket holders protested to the management, and, so the story goes, threatened to report the matter to the Board of Trade if the speed was not reduced. Nowadays, although the Caley and the Sou-West are both merged in the same group the tradition of those hectic competition days persists on the Clyde, in the smart running of the boat trains, in the slickness of transfer from rail to steamer, and in the incomparable navigating of the vessels themselves.

For three successive Januarys the annual Scottish number of *The Railway Magazine* was enriched by an article from the racy pen of Mr. David L. Smith: "G. & S.W. Nights Entertainments"; "More G. & S.W. Nights Entertainments"; and "Still More G & S.W. Nights Entertainments." While in these articles it is mainly the bizarre and the dramatic that is recorded there shines through all the unfailing devotion to duty of the train crews, sometimes in the face of almost overwhelming odds. Most of these episodes took place on the very hilly section of line between Ayr and Stranraer. And what a road! Gradients up to 1 in 54, like that of the Glendoune Bank starting straight off the platform end at Girvan; stretches of fast running switchback, as from Maybole southward to Girvan; and scenes like that going north from Pinmore, where there bursts into view suddenly the breath-taking spectacle of Ailsa Craig riding like some vast grape-blue phantom isle on the sparkling waters of the Firth of Clyde. Southward the railway climbs to the wild moorland summit of Chirmorie, and so down by heavy gradients to the yellow sands of Luce Bay, and a sight of the coast stretching far beyond to the Mull of Galloway.

The working of loose-coupled goods trains over such a road is an acquired art. After pounding up a heavy grade, like that to Maybole, you have two alternatives;

first to let the wagons close in, crawl down the next descent, and then pick up the couplings for the next ascending grade from a walking pace, or even a dead stop. Such a procedure would be very slow. Generally it is the second alternative that must be aimed at on a switchback road, namely to keep the couplings tight all the time. In this the driver and guard must co-operate, the guard by keeping his van brakes on during each descent, and the driver by running at such a speed as to keep ahead of the leading wagons; for it would be beyond the power of the guard's brake van to hold these wagons back.

The "Midnicht"—express goods from Glasgow to Stranraer—was a heavy train, and some forty years ago it needed to be double-headed every night over the heavy grades south of Ayr. Piloting the "Midnicht" was a great job for the young drivers of Ayr, keen young fellows just promoted, whose other duties were mostly humdrum, in the way of spare and local jobs. The regular driver from the Glasgow end was a staid old Scot called McLatchie, and the young men of Ayr used to vie with one another as to who could "assist" him the fastest. Well, one fine night Bob Duncan was pilot driver, he who years after became one of the crack drivers on the Ayr-Glasgow residential expresses. He had a quaint old engine of the 0–4–2 type, with no brakes at all on the engine and a hand brake with wooden blocks on the tender.

There was usually no other traffic about at that hour in the morning, and the "Midnicht" had the road to itself. What happened after Maybole is best described in Smith's own words: "They came thundering down Crosshill bank to find Kilkerran distant signal *red!* Shut off, screw the hand brake, whistle! Round the curve at the Secret Works and horrors here was the home signal, *red too*, and the gates across the line! Duncan whirled that reverser into back gear and flung full steam in her teeth. The old thing just about doubled up with him but they stopped—*inches* only from the gates. They then discovered that the signalman had *fallen asleep!"*

Another event that might have had alarming consequences ended, however, in pure comedy. A very heavy goods had to be taken southwards from Girvan; only one engine was available, and so the only way to tackle the 1 in 54 gradient of the Glendoune bank was to take half the train up first, leave those wagons at Pinmore station, return to Girvan for the second half, and couple up again when both halves had been conveyed to the summit. The first half climbed the bank all right and the engine had just got back to Girvan when Pinmore wired that the first half was "away"! "Away" meant just one thing, that those wagons, without any brake van to control them, were running away down the 1 in 70 gradient towards Pinwherry.

Gathering momentum they were soon in headlong flight, and dashed through Pinwherry at very nearly sixty miles per hour. Fortunately the gradient rises very steeply beyond this station, and after a mile or so their momentum was exhausted. Back they came again, roaring through Pinwherry, and up the opposite gradient towards Pinmore. So they continued, down one side and up the other, five or six times till they finally came to rest. The tit-bit of the whole affair was the comment the morning after of a permanent way inspector who happened to be staying the night at the Pinwherry station-house. He was emphatic that he had never tried to sleep at a busier country-station; there were, he declared, trains through the night every ten minutes.

The clocking of train speeds must often have been voted the strangest of all pastimes, for it is one in which amateur railway enthusiasts must necessarily pursue their hobby in full view of the travelling public. The historian, the photographer, the Bradshaw fan, and the collector of tickets can, and mostly do, make themselves quite inconspicuous; but it would take more than a master of camouflage to operate a split-second chronograph for long in a compartment full of people without exciting the curiosity, and sometimes the open derision of some fellow traveller. As one who has recorded train speeds in this way for the past twenty-five years I have had many such encounters—some very amusing and one, during the Autumn of 1940, in which the interested party did his level best to get me arrested as a dangerous suspect! But I must first of all tell of the late Charles Rous-Marten, doyen of this corps of—well, some would call us quaint people.

Rous-Marten was Editor of the *New Zealand Times*, but in between his duties as such he managed to do an extraordinary amount of railway travelling. Through his writings in the engineering press of the day, he came to be an acknowledged authority on locomotive working and train speeds in general. At the time of the Race to Aberdeen, August 1895, he must have been working a 24-hour day. In the company of a band of fellow enthusiasts, and armed with four watches—one in each hand,

and one in each trousers pocket—he would clock the racing of the 8 a.m. sleeping car express from King's Cross throughout the night. Then, as the flyer was coasting into Aberdeen, Rous-Marten dressed in a black frock coat and tall hat would leap from the carriage, race across the platform and board the morning London express just as it was starting away. On one such occasion he was assisted into the southbound train by an astonished guard, who remarked somewhat drily: "Ye'll no be making a long stay in Aberdeen the morrn".

Rous-Marten never varied his picturesque attire, even on those occasions when he was privileged to travel on the locomotives themselves, and on one occasion his striking appearance brought upon him the quite undeserved wrath of a train load of passengers. Setting out to test a new Midland engine between St. Pancras and Leicester, the crew were early in difficulties. The engine started to prime, that is, water passed direct from the boiler to the cylinders, and nothing would stop it. For nearly 100 miles they floundered along with intermittent showers of oily black liquid from the chimney; and the train arrived at Leicester not merely late but with the leading carriages fairly plastered. Irate passengers seeing so imposing a dignitary on the footplate naturally descended upon him like a cloud.

Train timing, if it is to yield an accurate record, needs a certain amount of concentration, and an empty compartment is the stop-watcher's ideal. One afternoon in the summer of 1927 I was travelling from Leamington to Paddington by the "Shakespeare Express". It was a fast train and I was bent on taking a fairly complete record of the running. I was just congratulating myself on finding an empty compartment, when at the very last minute, in dashed no fewer than six American ladies, who had been "doing" the Shakespeare country. The day had been gloriously fine; the sights they had seen were terrific, and to one and all life was simply just great. The Great Western driver evidently thought that these distinguished visitors should have their day's trip properly concluded, for we were soon piling on some tremendous speed. But I noticed that amid the torrent of joyous conversation there were numerous sidelong glances at my stop-watch, and I began to fear the worst.

The blow fell just as we were beginning a record-breaking ascent of the Chiltern Hills. Then, the youngest, and certainly not the least attractive of my travelling companions leaned across the compartment "Excuse me", she said, "but what are you doing with that watch?" It was useless to explain that I was measuring the speed. The whole party joined in, and bombarded me with questions. "How did I do it?" "Where were the mile posts?" The stop-watch was passed from one to another. They crowded round the window. Amid shrieks of delight they started and stopped the watch "Say, Eleanor, you try; I can't see any mile posts at arl." Then, at me, "How do you see the mile posts at night?" Little by little, the intricacies of rail-joint timing had to be explained, and we were nearing the outer suburbs of London before their questions ceased. Then the youngest, and I repeat, not the least attractive of them aptly summed up the situation with "Well, you sure have been ca-ancentratin'!"

Since the war broke out my own travelling has been

very much reduced, and, in any case, the slowing down of train schedules has made the running of considerably less interest. So it happened that journeys made when my children were young were not usually complicated by a desire on my part to record the locomotive work. There was, however, one amusing exception. Joining a north-bound express at Exeter in the early summer of 1943 we were lucky enough to find an empty compartment. The load was heavy, and the engine a famous veteran, and I was curious to see what kind of speed we would make. At first all went well; the running was good, so were the children, doing full justice to a delectable wartime tea.

But after Taunton, though my own interest quickened, my son, then aged one-and-a-half years, grew distinctly bored with the whole business. With the locomotive going great guns my attention had perforce to be divided —a stop-watch in one hand, the other producing a hand-kerchief, conjuror fashion, from various unexpected parts of my person to the huge enjoyment of my offspring. We were approaching an important junction, and the speed was still rising, when my daughter, aged five, decided to assist in the entertainment. She too produced a handker-chief and tossed it gaily into the air; and since the window was wide open and the air-current strong, that handkerchief was wafted equally gaily outside. Amid the laughter and tears that greeted this disappearing trick he for whom the entertainment had been devised showed his approval by falling off the seat! Our passing time at that important junction went unrecorded.

It is not only devotees of the timing art who like to travel alone. We are, on the whole, a nation of most unsociable travellers, a trait that Mr. Punch has recorded in a memorable cartoon. Yet there are times when our travelling habits swing to the very opposite extreme. I remember an occasion when the close approach of an important seven-a-side Rugger tournament suggested a Sunday afternoon practice for the two "sevens" we were entering; and with referee, coach, and other well-wishers a party of nineteen strong mustered at King's Cross. Station and train were alike almost deserted, yet to the astonishment of a solitary platform inspector our whole party piled into one non-corridor compartment! All might have been well, but for the indiscretion of one supporter in turning out in a bowler, which before the train had emerged from the first tunnel out of King's Cross was being used for a bout of passing practice. Within the confines of that compartment, and with a breathless pause at each intermediate station, the rag went fast and furious until our arrival at an outer suburban station, where a wing three-quarter of some reputation was seen sprinting the length of the platform in his stockinged feet after a miscreant who was away with his shoes.

There seems to be no end to the uses of old railway carriages. They serve as caravan coaches for holiday-makers, sleeping quarters for Engineers Department men working on isolated parts of the line, where lodgings would be difficult to obtain, and, shorn of their wheels, these old vehicles may be seen doing duty as shunters' cabins, railway canteens, and even dwelling houses. Mr. W. Heath Robinson, in his book *Railway Ribaldry* has suggested a most picturesque use for old—very old—locomotive boilers: up-end them with the fire-box end downwards, whereupon the long chimney makes an excellent support for a children's swing! This is a much happier alternative to the inglorious scrap heap. But the most extraordinary invention for the use of old rolling stock stands to the credit of the G.W.R. locomotive department, and it dates from 1887, the year of Queen Victoria's Golden Jubilee.

Swindon's part in the loyal celebration of the Jubilee took the form of a huge fête and tea in New Swindon Park. Some 15,000 people were expected to attend, and the problem arose as to how to make the vast quantity of tea that the multitude was expected to imbibe. Clearly it was a task calling for a supreme feat of organization; and in Swindon what body was more fitted to undertake it than the Locomotive Department of the G.W.R.? And undertake it they did in a way that for sheer originality eclipses some achievements of the great Brunel himself. They boiled the tea in old locomotive tenders! After some intensive scouring out three or four tenders were put into a siding near to the park and filled with cold water; then cases of tea were emptied into the tanks. An old locomotive had been stationed alongside, and from this a flexible pipe was connected to each of the tenders in turn, and live steam blown in to boil the water. The tenders had previously been fitted with taps, and from these relay after relay of tea urns were replenished.

And now I come to a story of heroism on the railway, which serves to show the deep sense of responsibility and instinctive regard for the safety of traffic which is found among members of the service when exceptional circumstances arise.

During the week-end of June 20th and 21st, 1936, in the Newtown district of Montgomeryshire, events moved like the scenario of an American screen melodrama than happenings on a British railway. The whole of England was swept by storms of great violence, but in these Welsh hills both rain and thunder were of an almost tropical intensity. Conditions were bad enough on the Saturday, when the river Severn overflowed and Newtown itself was flooded, but so far the railway had suffered no harm. Through this district the main line of the one time Cambrian railways, later part of the G.W.R., follows the Severn valley, and it carries a heavy holiday traffic to the Cambrian Coast resorts.

Late on the Sunday afternoon things were beginning to look ugly at Scafell, a hamlet some two miles west of Newtown. The tiny station here is one of the few in charge of a station-mistress, and the lady in question was the wife of a retired permanent way man, ex-Ganger Haynes. At 6 p.m. the thunderstorms culminated in a terrific cloudburst in the hills south of the Severn valley, which caused the rivers to rise so rapidly that Haynes feared for the safety of the railway. It was not the Severn that seemed the most potential source of danger, but the Dulais river, which comes down from the very hills where the cloudburst had taken place. So, at the height of the storm, Haynes and his daughter went out to keep watch at the bridge.

Just at the point where the Dulais enters the Severn it is crossed by the railway, running on a 20 ft. embankment, the foot of which is washed on the north side by the waters of the Severn. At that time the bridge over the

212

Dulais river was a solid masonry structure with an arch of 25 ft. span. When Haynes and his daughter arrived on the scene the neighbouring fields were already flooded, and the little river, normally nothing more than a turbulent mountain stream, was a really terrifying sight. A great volume of water was sweeping down, carrying all before it; bushes along the banks were being torn up as if they were tender seedlings, and the force of this onrush was scouring out the banks and bringing great pressure on the abutments of the railway bridge.

Dulais Farmhouse, just on the Newtown side of the river, was completely marooned, the ground floor rooms being flooded to a depth of five or six feet; and in the hope of being able to help the unfortunate people there Haynes and his daughter crossed the railway bridge. They were hardly over when a still more unexpected thing happened. On the Scafell side of the Dulais river was a group of huge venerable elms; under the tremendous winds these were waving like so many reeds, when suddenly one of them was completely uprooted by the rush of water. By some extraordinary freak of wind and water it was borne down stream in a perfectly upright position, and a few seconds later had crashed into the railway bridge. It struck the parapet, which was at once destroyed; the tree rebounded, and was then dragged under the arch by the force of the current. Its passage ripped away the crown of the arch, and immediately the whole bridge collapsed. A curious point noted by Haynes was that the downstream side of the arch fell in first.

The telegraph wires were undamaged, and at once Haynes thought of the up mail, which had already left

213

Aberystwyth. Between them and the telephone at Scafell station was a breach in the line 60 ft. long, across which the tracks were suspended in mid-air. The only thing to do was to go to Newtown and send warning from there. The storm was now if possible worse than ever, and yet, amid darkness almost of night, in torrents of rain and incessant thunder, Miss Haynes set out to walk two miles down the line to give the alarm. It was by no means certain that she could get through. The way might easily be barred by floods or another washaway; so Haynes attempted to get back to his home by way of the road, which runs parallel to the railway and about a quarter of a mile away. By going a short distance from the course of the river he was able to wade across the flooded fields, and eventually he got to the road. This also was under water, but he managed to cross the river. He was hardly over when this bridge too was swept away. All the time the mail train was getting nearer. There are no signals at Scafell, and the bridge is approached on a curve from a deep cutting; speed is usually 50 to 55 m.p.h. at this point, and travelling thus on a day of poor visibility the driver would never be able to see the breach in time. But when at last Haynes reached his home and telephoned through to Caersws, the next station open, he learned that his daughter had been in time and the train was stopped.

But even now that tragedy was averted the task of these plucky folk was not ended. Sunday evening is proverbially a bad time to find people in a hurry, but Haynes managed to get into telephone communication with the Bridge Foreman at Caersws, and from his own railway experience was able to tell him the exact nature of the washaway. This was of no little help later in the evening when plans were made for bridging the gap. And then, as if he had not rendered enough service, Haynes went out on the main road to warn motorists of the broken bridge, and continued to do so until 2 o'clock next morning.

These occasions of hold-up, and mischance, are, in their very rarity, fascinating to hear about and study; but to conclude with such an episode might tend to leave an impression of hazard, instead of that incomparable record of safe working which is one of the most prized possessions of the British railways. But even at the Dulais bridge, danger though there was in plenty, it is not the danger, nor yet the extraordinary circumstances in which the bridge was destroyed, that remain most vivid among the many impressions left by the whole affair. It is the manifestation of the railway tradition, the tradition of service, that renders the Dulais incident so deeply impressive. It was the same railway tradition which brought three senior engineers into urgent conference late on that wild Sunday night; they worked swiftly, and ere they turned in, plans had been made for bridging the gap, and the necessary materials ordered from head-quarters by telegram. In less dramatic moments the railway tradition is to be seen in the quiet disciplined service rendered year in, year out in signal boxes, in marshalling yards, on the footplate, and indeed wherever there are trains—in fair weather and foul, in peace and war.

The railways of Britain have always been proud of

their traditions, traditions which have been handed down through more than a hundred years of service, and enriched by successive generations of men who have given their life's work to the making, enlarging and operating of the great network covering the country today. Even though the railways are passing through a period of great stress and anxiety, we as a nation should not cease to be proud of this great heritage.

Index

The numerals in bold type refer to the *figure numbers* of the illustrations

218

219

220

221

223